THE PHYSICIAN ASSISTANT:

An Illustrated History

Thomas E. Piemme, MD
Alfred M. Sadler, Jr., MD
Reginald D. Carter, PhD, PA
Ruth Ballweg, MPA, PA-C

Sponsored by the Physician Assistant History Society

Acacia Publishing, Inc.
Gilbert, Arizona

This book made possible in part by funds granted by the Robert Wood Johnson Foundation and the Josiah Macy Jr. Foundation.

The statements made and views expressed are solely the responsibility of the authors.

Address inquiries to: Physician Assistant History Society, 12000 Findley Road, Ste. 100, Johns Creek, GA (ContactUs@pahx.org)

Library of Congress Control Number: 2013906837

ISBN 978-1-935089-64-3

Published by
Acacia Publishing, Inc.
Gilbert, Arizona
www.acaciapublishing.com

Printed and Bound in the United States of America

First Printing May 2013
Second Printing June 2013
Third Printing April 2018

TO ALL OF THE PAs WHOSE DEDICATION TO CLINICAL EXCELLENCE IN THE CARE OF PATIENTS HAS MADE THE PROFESSION THE GREAT SUCCESS THAT IT IS TODAY.

TABLE OF CONTENTS

PREFACE

The Physician Assistant History Society website (pahx.org) is a rich source of information about the history of the Physician Assistant profession. It has been built with loving care over a decade, diligently maintained, and regularly expanded and updated. It receives thousands of "hits" each month.

Using the website, it is possible to gain a deep knowledge of the people, places, and events of the half century of remarkable growth and development of this new health occupation. PA students are required by the "Standards" of accreditation to be informed about the history of the profession they are entering. But it isn't always easy or convenient. The critical elements of the website are the "Timeline" of events, the biographies of notable people who have advanced the profession, and the images associated with both. But the internet is not a linear medium. In order to navigate the story, one must use the "links" that are imbedded in the Timeline.

As the authors sat in the new offices of the History Society last fall, it occurred to us that the information might well be collated, expanded upon, and presented in another medium that would be intrinsically more linear: A Timeline handbook, punctuated with images, and brief biographies of the major contributors to the events. If offered at a reasonable price, it might serve as a textbook and/or a ready reference within a course of the study of the history of the profession.

As the authors began to assemble the material, other opportunities presented themselves. The members of the profession have been, from the outset, creative people who have had remarkable success, both within and outside the profession itself. We have seen PAs appointed to state and Federal advisory boards, promoted to flag officer status in the military services, appointed to chair state medical boards, and one, elected to Congress. Some have written books, published seminal articles, achieved professorial rank in academic institutions, and headed international relief delegations. Realizing that many of these achievements were unrecognized in the Timeline, we elected to cite some of the more unique accomplishments at the end of each decade. These PAs are not necessarily the leaders of the governing organizations; those are recognized in the lists of elected officers in Appendix A. Certainly many more PAs could have been included. The choices are meant to be representative, and are those of the authors collectively.

Similarly, there have been scores of professionals, who are not PAs, who have championed the profession, and provided opportunity for the profession to become established, and grow. We have expressed our appreciation to a selected number of these in Appendix B. Again, the choices are from among many who could have been included, and are those of the authors.

While we hope that this book will serve effectively both as a primer, and as a reference for PA students, it should be of interest to a large number of the more than 105,000 PAs who have graduated from 170 programs, and been initially certified by the NCCPA. We expect that it might well be of interest to many others, as well. In particular, it could provide an introduction to the profession to high school and college students who have not yet settled on a choice of a career, and to the guidance counselors who advise them. There are those in the general public, whom we hope might gain a better understanding of who PAs are, and what they do. Finally, this book should be useful to members of other health professions, and health policy makers, who are charged with enhancing access to high quality medical care. To that end, it will be made broadly available in bookstores around the nation, and on the internet.

Thomas E. Piemme
Alfred M. Sadler, Jr.
Reginald D. Carter
Ruth Ballweg

Acknowledgments

While attributed to four authors, this book is, in reality, the product of the Physician Assistant History Society. It is in large part a derivative work. The Society was formed a decade ago in order to collect, archive, catalog, and preserve documents, images, video- and audiotapes, and other artifacts of the history of the profession. Under the management of Reginald Carter, the Executive Director until his retirement four years ago, and currently Historian Emeritus, the website of the History Society was built, and then enhanced with advice and encouragement from the many Trustees who have served on the Board of Directors over the years.

The signature element of the website is the "Timeline." Inspired by a timeline in the textbook by Rod Hooker and Jim Cawley, Carter has created an extraordinary resource. Built painstakingly with input from the major PA organizations, the American Academy of Physician Assistants, the Physician Assistant Education Association, the National Commission on Certification of Physician Assistants, and the Accreditation Review Commission on Education for the Physician Assistant, it stands as uniquely rich history of the profession. We are deeply indebted to the members of the staff of the four organizations who provided much of the raw material.

Although begun as an independent entity, the History Society has found a home as an affiliate organization to the NCCPA. We are exceedingly grateful for the encouragement and generous financial support of the Board of Directors of the Commission. Specifically, we thank Pam Dean, the Interim President and CEO of the NCCPA for her support, and most especially, Lori Konopka-Sauer for editorial assistance, and Keri Caudill for her graphic design. Without them this book would not have been possible.

We are grateful to the Robert Wood Johnson Foundation and the Josiah Macy, Jr. foundation for their support in our effort to seek source documents from archives of the many organizations that contributed to the founding of the PA profession. Appreciation is extended to Blair Sadler for his review and commentary on the policy aspects of the first and last chapters of the book.

Finally, we sincerely thank Karen Gray, President of Acacia Publishing, for her editorial assistance, and her colleague Jason Crye for his diligent efforts in formatting the elements of the final product.

T.E.P., A.M.S., Jr., R.D.C. and R.B.

Glossary of Acronyms

AAFP	American Academy of Family Practice
AAMC	Association of American Medical Colleges
AAP	American Academy of Pediatrics
AAP	American Academy of Physician Assistants
ACGME	Accreditation Council on Graduate Medical Education
ACP	American College of Physicians
ACS	American College of Surgeons
AHA	American Hospital Association
AHRQ	Agency for Healthcare Research and Quality
AMA	American Medical Association
ANA	American Nurses Association
APAP	Association of Physician Assistant Programs
ARC-PA	Accreditation Review Commission on Education for the Physician Assistant
ARPA	American Registry of Physicians' Associates
ASIM	American Society for Internal Medicine

CAHEA	Council on Allied Health Education and Accreditation
CAQ	Certificate of Added Qualifications
CASPA	Central Application Service for Physician Assistants
CHA	Child Health Associate
DHEW	Department of Health Education and Welfare
DHHS	Department of Health and Human Services
FSMB	Federation of State Medical Boards
GMENAC	Graduate Medical Education National Advisory Committee
GRADRAT	Graduate Rating Assessment Tool
HOD	House of Delegates (AAPA)
HRSA	Health Resources and Services Administration
IOM	Institute of Medicine
IPAP	Interservice Physician Assistant Program
JAAPA	Journal of the American Academy of Physician Assistants
JCAHO	Joint Commission on Accreditation of Healthcare Organizations
JPAEA	Journal of the Physician Assistant Education Association
JRC-PA	Joint Review Committee for Educational Programs for the Physician Assistant
MEDEX	Model of PA education originated by Richard Smith, MD (MEDicine EXtension)
NBME	National Board of Medical Examiners
NCCPA	National Commission on Certification of Physician Assistants
NLN	National League for Nursing
NP	Nurse Practitioner
PA	Physician Assistant (Physician Associate, used briefly in 1970's)
PAEA	Physician Assistant Education Association
PAHx	Physician Assistant History Society
PANCE	PA National Certifying Examination
PANRE	PA National Recertification Examination

PNP	Pediatric Nurse Practitioner
RWJF	Robert Wood Johnson Foundation
SPPAHx	Society for the Preservation of Physician Assistant History
USPHS	United States Public Health Service
WHO	World Health Organization

SETTING THE STAGE

How did it come to pass that, in less than 50 years, there have been more than 105,000 physician assistants (PAs) certified to practice medicine, when none existed before? More than 90,000 are actively practicing today. There are more than 170 accredited educational programs. The PA Master's degree is regarded as the most valuable Master's degree in the economy. PAs consistently report high job satisfaction. In studies of quality of care and patient satisfaction PAs, after two years of intensive training, perform favorably when compared with house officers and practicing physicians. Who are the people who make up this remarkable new profession? How did it happen? Although there have been scattered precedents for the use of non-physicians to provide care in other countries, and rare instances in the United States, the following story describes the unfolding of a new health profession that many claim to be one of the greatest innovations of the last half of the 20th century.

A TIME OF COURAGEOUS CHANGE AND INNOVATION

The 1960s were a time of great social upheaval. Issues of war, poverty, and racism racked the nation, amid riots and assassinations. Legislation to redress injustice and social inequality included the adoption of Medicare and Medicaid to ensure adequate health care for the aged and the poor. The nation's health care system was woefully unprepared. Advances in medical science following World War II led to a sharp increase in physician specialization at the expense of the broader practice of what would come to be called "primary care." Already in short supply, the number of physicians available to provide basic services to these newly enfranchised patients could not possibly meet the demand.

Two national commissions were convened, resulting in recommendations that led to the creation of the new specialty of Family Medicine (as the alternative to "general practice"), and the development of sections of General Internal Medicine and General Pediatrics within those respective academic departments. While these actions did lead eventually to the production of more primary care physicians, the intrinsic length of medical education precluded any effective rapid deployment.

At the same time, a number of leaders began to articulate what most physicians already knew: much of what the doctor does each day could be carried out by specially trained non-physicians, working alongside doctors as part of a team. Most physicians were already training office personnel to do more than answer the phone and schedule patients. In the "back office" they took vital signs, gathered information, and even performed minor procedures. (In developing countries, non-physicians had been doing this, and more, for centuries.) There was the remarkable example of United States military corpsmen, who with only a few months of training, were highly successful in managing battlefield injuries and illnesses. Their vital skills were lost to society when the corpsman was discharged from military service. Could these skills be harnessed to serve the civilian population in this country? The answer was to be a resounding Yes. New models of medical education for non-physicians were soon to emerge.

FORMAL EDUCATION AND TRAINING MODELS

At Duke University in the late 1950s, Thelma Ingles, RN, took a sabbatical year from the nursing school to work with Eugene A. Stead, Jr., MD, Chair of the Department of Medicine, to learn clinical medicine from him and his colleagues. Impressed with what nurses might be able to do, Ingles and Stead drew up a curriculum for "advanced clinical nursing" that would be offered to outstanding nurses who wanted to broaden their knowledge in a program leading to a Master's Degree in Nursing. The program was launched successfully, resulting in nurse clinicians with skills previously unknown in nursing. Ingles and Stead eagerly applied to the National League for Nursing for accreditation. To their stunned amazement this innovative program was rejected (twice). The two reasons given were that first, there was too much physician involvement in the curriculum, and, second, Ms. Ingles lacked a baccalaureate degree in nursing. (Her baccalaureate was in English from UCLA;

her nursing training had been in the outstanding three year diploma program at the Massachusetts General Hospital.) An opportunity for socially useful nurse/physician collaborative education, which might have been emulated elsewhere, was lost.

In 1960, Charles Hudson, MD, an emerging leader in the AMA, delivered an address to the House of Delegates in which he proposed that returning military corpsmen be provided with training to enhance their already formidable skills, in order to serve as assistants to practicing physicians. Somewhat surprisingly, the proposal was enthusiastically received by the medical profession when it was published in JAMA.

Stead was no stranger to the training of non-physicians to provide medical care. At Emory University during World War II, he used medical students (called "externs") to provide medical care on the wards in place of interns and residents who had been drafted into military service. He was well acquainted with Amos Johnson, MD, a respected general practitioner in rural North Carolina, who had trained a young farm boy to be his assistant, and to treat patients in his absence when he was away. Stead had observed former corpsmen working in the laboratories of his faculty colleagues, performing specialized procedures with patients. In 1964 he announced that he intended to create, the following year, a course of study for corpsmen to become "physician's assistants."

In 1965, four former Navy Corpsmen entered a two year program at Duke University that included nine months of training in basic medical sciences, and fifteen months of clinical rotations. Three of the candidates graduated two years later.

Concurrently in 1965, at the University of Colorado, Henry A. Silver, MD, and Loretta Ford, RN, EdD, collaborated to develop a four month "Pediatric Nurse Practitioner" program, training skilled nurses to provide well baby care, and manage the more common outpatient pediatric illnesses. Recognizing that much more of primary care pediatrics could be treated by non-physicians, Silver went on to create a two year program which, followed by a year of internship, led to the Master's degree as a "Child Health Associate." He then worked closely with the state legislature to change the Colorado Medical Practice Act to permit these "Associates" to "practice pediatrics," if working with, and under the supervision of, a pediatrician.

In Seattle, Richard Smith, MD, started his own variation of an assistant to the physician, whom he called MEDEX. Having worked in the Indian Health Service, and with the Peace Corps in Nigeria, Smith recognized that non-physicians could play a crucial role in caring for the underserved in rural locations. Opening in 1969 at the University of Washington, the program focused first on building the skills of former career military corpsmen, and then placing them in an apprentice relationship with a primary care physician in a rural location, in one of the four states in the upper-Northwest. It was his expectation that, upon graduation, the MEDEX would be employed by his mentor.

Two other models, developed in the late 1960s, are worthy of note. John Kirklin, MD, Chair of Surgery at the University of Alabama, launched a "Surgeon's Assistant" program under the direction of his wife, Margaret, also a surgeon. Hu Myers, MD, a surgeon in rural West Virginia with his own hospital, collaborated with Alderson Broaddus, a liberal arts college in Phillipi, WV, to create a four year baccalaureate program to train students from the region to become physician assistants. Both programs succeeded, adding to the momentum for the concept of training non-physician providers to extend the reach of physicians.

The programs developed at Duke University and at the University of Washington received wide national attention, and were quickly emulated at several academic medical centers. Two important questions remained: Would the assistant to the physician be widely accepted by the medical community? Would states permit them to practice medicine, even under the supervision of a physician?

FRAMING EFFECTIVE LEGISLATION

The time-honored mode of state regulation of health occupations had been *licensure*. It is the process by which a state grants permission to persons, meeting predetermined qualifications, to engage in an occupation and/or use a particular title. The physician assistant appeared on the scene at a time when the system of licensure was being viewed by many as a means of protecting the occupation from competition, rather than protecting the public from unethical or incompetent practitioners. The abuses of licensure were assailed by reports from both the American Medical Association and the American Hospital Association in 1970. The Federal government agreed. The Department of HEW urged a moratorium on the licensing of new health occupations until such time as improvements in criteria could be made. The only alternative to licensure for the physician assistant was an amendment to the medical practice act, permitting the PA to work under the "supervision, control, and responsibility" of the licensed physician.

The first state to amend its medical practice act was California. Although a useful beginning, the legislation was flawed in two respects. First, it attempted to delineate the tasks that the PA was permitted to perform. Secondly, it added language detailing requirements of the programs from which PAs might graduate. With respect to the first issue, it was becoming apparent to educators that tasks that might be assigned to PAs were almost limitless. Far preferable was legislation that would permit the supervising physician to assign any task for which the PA had been trained, providing that the task was within the scope of practice of the physician. Such "delegatory" amendments quickly became the standard for almost all of the states that followed. With respect to the second issue, educational standards were far better left to some recognized national body that could accredit programs.

ACCREDITATION OF EMERGING PHYSICIAN ASSISTANT PROGRAMS

Following the pilot program at Duke University, and the attendant favorable publicity, programs purporting to train assistants to physicians exploded around the country. They varied in length from several weeks to four years. They were sponsored by proprietary companies, as well as academic medical centers. Private physicians even attempted to train them. A first attempt at rationalization was made by the National Academy of Sciences. PA Training was classified into three categories (Types A, B, and C) based upon length and depth of training, and upon whether the program was intended to produce generalist or specialist assistants. While thought-provoking, the classification did little to address quality, or identify specific programs in a useful way.

Accreditation is defined as the process by which an agency or organization evaluates and recognizes a program of study as meeting certain predetermined qualifications or standards. In 1971, in a manner analogous to the criticism being leveled at licensure, the processes of educational accreditation were being charged with perpetuating a "credentials monopoly" in a report prepared for DHEW by Prof. Frank Newman of Stanford University. The "Newman Report" urged that there was a need to "open up alternative routes to obtaining credentials." The report was very useful in establishing the principles of accreditation and certification of PAs.

Upon urging from PA program directors, and the Federation of State Medical Boards, the AMA took the lead in accreditation of PA programs. The AMA had a long history of accrediting allied health education through its Committee on Allied Health Professions and Services. C.H. William Ruhe, MD, PhD, Director of Medical Education at the AMA, formed a committee that included representatives of specialty societies in internal medicine, pediatrics and family medicine, as well as the Association of American Medical Colleges. The product of deliberation was a document entitled, "Essentials for Educational Programs for the Assistant to the Primary Care Physician." Adopted overwhelmingly by the House of Delegates in 1971, it led directly to the establishment of the Joint Review Committee for Educational Programs for the Assistant to the Primary Care Physician (JRC-PA). Accreditation of PA programs began in 1972. Highlights of its progress over 40 years appear in the following chapters of this book.

CERTIFICATION OF PROGRAM GRADUATES

Certification is the process by which a nongovernmental agency grants recognition to an individual who has met predetermined qualifications specified by that agency. It serves the public interest as a check on educational programs and the accreditation process, and must be independent. In 1972, the National Board of Medical Examiners stepped forward to assume that responsibility. (It was the first time the NBME had been involved in the examination of any health professionals other than physicians.) The first examination was administered in December of 1973.

The NBME, a highly respected testing agency, was uncomfortable with assuming the additional roles of determining which candidates might be eligible to take the examination, and establishing the cut-off score that would qualify the candidate to practice as a physician assistant. In 1974, in unprecedented collaboration, a meeting of fourteen national organizations was convened by Malcolm C. Todd, MD, Chair of the AMA Council on Health Manpower, in order to establish a National Commission on Certification of Physician Assistants (NCCPA). Its charge would be to assume the roles of determining eligibility and standards for the examination, and to issue certificates that could be used by the states to identify qualified PAs. The NCCPA had broad representation from relevant medical specialties, Federal and state agencies, nursing, educational programs, and practicing PAs. It included public members, as well, conforming in almost every particular to the criteria for legitimacy that had been articulated by the Newman Report.

ORGANIZING THE PROFESSION

During this formative period, two essential professional organizations were established. In April of 1968 the students and graduates of the Duke University program formed the American Association of Physician's Assistants, incorporating it in North Carolina. Within three years the officers recruited membership from graduates beyond the local community, elected new leadership from around the nation, and gained recognition as the sole voice for the profession. It became the American Academy of Physician Assistants.

Absent any national system of identifying persons who might be considered "legitimate," trained physician assistants, leaders of the early programs collaborated in 1970 to establish the American Registry of Physician's Associates in order to recognize graduates of the "Type A" programs. By early 1972 it had become clear that both accreditation and certification were on the horizon. In April, 1972 those pioneering programs, now numbering fourteen, decided to dissolve the Registry. Recognizing that they had common issues, they formed the Association of Physician Assistant Programs, allowing fruitful collaboration on such matters as admission criteria, curriculum design, clinical preceptorships, role delineation, faculty training, and continuing medical education.

Both AAPA and APAP relied, at first, upon voluntary leadership. Communication and effective functioning were dependent upon the time availability of the elected officers. In the summer of 1973, Alfred M. Sadler, Jr. MD and Thomas E. Piemme, MD, Past President, and President, respectively, of APAP successfully sought and received sufficient private foundation funds to establish a joint national office in Washington, DC. They recruited Donald W. Fisher, PhD, to serve as Executive Director of both organizations. Full time staff was now available to advance the interest of the PA movement, and most vitally, to serve as a resource for the states as they revised their medical practice statutes. While some conflicts emerged, common management served to promote cohesion of interest between education and practice.

A NATIONAL CONFERENCE OF CONVERGENT INTERESTS

Between 1968 and 1972 Duke University hosted four invitational conferences to provide a forum for the exchange of experiences and ideas among existing and emerging programs. At the fourth of these gatherings in April, 1972, Duke suggested that the time had come for national organizations to carry on what they had started. The leadership of AAPA and APAP promptly began planning for a national conference to be held in April, 1973. Since no funds were available, the PA program at Sheppard Air Force Base offered to host the meeting at its facilities in Wichita Falls, TX, and the Air Force willingly advanced the necessary "seed money" until registration fees were received.

The conference was billed as the "First Annual Conference on New Health Practitioners" in the hope that there might be substantial participation by the growing number of nurse practitioners. Few nurses attended, however. The Conference proved ultimately to be the first of the annual meetings of the AAPA.

While there were presentations on emerging legal issues, and reports of early studies of PA utilization and cost effectiveness, the highlights of the meeting were the presentations by the NBME and the AMA. The first national certifying examination was only a few months away, and JRC-PA now had a year of experience with accreditation of programs. Those who attended the meeting came away, reassured that the PA concept was healthy, and would endure.

DEPENDENCE VS. INDEPENDENCE, AND THE EVOLUTION OF THE ROLE OF THE PHYSICIAN ASSISTANT

Although Hudson, Stead, Smith, and other pioneers of the PA concept initially envisioned the role of the PA primarily as a data gatherer, performing somewhat limited, but repetitive tasks (the common phrase among them was, "extending the arms and legs of the physician"), it quickly became apparent that the PA could do much more. Given the prior experience of the students, most of whom had been military corpsmen, clinical evaluation and treatment of injuries were a natural fit. Add to that the skills of history-taking and physical examination, and the evolution into diagnosing, treating, operating and prescribing was natural and inevitable. Working under the supervision of physicians, a diligent PA can, over time, master much of the scope of practice of his, or her, mentors. Without question within a few years of the introduction of the concept, PAs were, in effect practicing medicine.

Although both accreditation and certification were designed for the "assistant to the primary care physician," it wasn't long before some PAs gravitated to the specialties. PAs do what physicians do, and they will practice what physicians practice. Today PAs function in roles unimagined in the 1960s and 1970s. PAs were described in 1975 by Sadler, Sadler, and Bliss as "the human equivalent of a new technology." Technology evolves. And so has the physician assistant.

Given that PAs do indeed practice medicine, there has been, from time to time, an argument proffered by some that the PA might well function independently. Stead was forthright from the outset, when he said that, as long as PAs remain legally dependent upon the physician, there is no limit to their scope of practice. If they were to move to practice independently, their scope of practice would be circumscribed and limited by the medical profession, and state licensing boards.

As the MD/PA team becomes comfortable working together in practice, they achieve mutual respect, and the PA does indeed "function independently" in many ways. As the MD and PA accrue new knowledge, they often teach each other. The dependence/independence issue becomes moot. They have evolved to *interdependence*.

The following graphs show the dramatic growth in the number of PAs that have been certified over the years, and the number of programs that have been accredited.

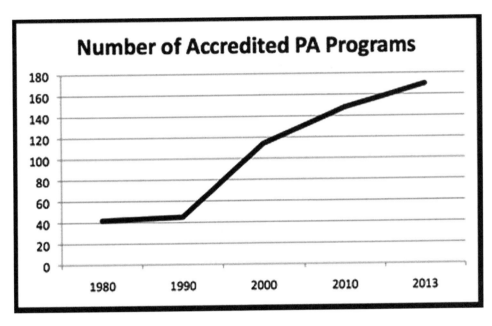

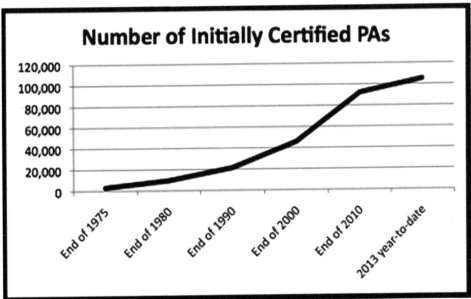

In the chapters that follow, we present a timeline of people, places and events that have shaped the Physician Assistant profession.

1650–1956

Historic Precedents

Providing medical care to remote populations where none existed, and meeting military and public health needs, have been concerns of nations for centuries. The use of non-physicians to provide health care services has an extensive history. Among the more noteworthy experiments were efforts to deliver services to the Russian wilderness, to the communes of rural China, to the frontiers of the American West, and to native-American villages in Alaska. Military necessity, especially in times of war, led to the use of non-physicians to provide acute care at army bases, and on warships in France, England, and post-revolutionary America. The United States Public Health Service found a need to use former military corpsmen in prisons. Advanced, highly technical surgical procedures, developed in mid-20th century, led innovators to train technicians to assist in urology and cardiovascular surgery. In the 1940s a unique event took place. A highly respected general practitioner in rural North Carolina trained his own "doctor's assistant" to care for his patients, even while he was away to further his medical education. Remarkably, that partnership received great praise from organized medicine. A road had been mapped; it was soon to be paved by pioneer educators.

1650

Feldshers, originally German military medical assistants (field surgeons, or "barber surgeons"), are introduced into **Russian armies** by Peter the Great in the 17th Century. Feldshers continue to practice in modern Russia and are used to provide primary, preventive and maternity care services in rural areas.

1778

An enlisted man, John Wall, is assigned by the US Navy as a **"loblolly boy"** to assist medical officers on the **USS Constellation**. One year later, Congress passes a bill authorizing the Navy to use hospital mates, modeled after the "loblolly boys" of the British Royal Navy, to assist physicians in the care of sailors. In the 1800s the name is changed to "surgeon's steward," then to "apothecary," and again to "bayman." In the early 20th century they become Hospital Corpsmen.

1803

"Officiers de Sante" are introduced in **France** by Rene Fourcroy to help alleviate health personnel shortages in both military and civilian sectors (abolished in 1892).

Introduced in the 17th century, Feldshers provide care to rural communities, even in modern times.

John Wall is the first 'Loblolly Boy" assigned to a US Navy frigate, the USS Constellation.

President McKinley signs legislation in 1898, establishing the US Navy Hospital Corps. From then to the present day, medical servicemen in the Navy have been called "hospital corpsmen."

1863

Johanna Maria Hedén, a midwife, becomes the first known licensed female feldsher (barber surgeon) and, as such, the first known formally educated and trained female surgeon in **Sweden**.

1891

Capt. John Van Renssalaer Hoff, MC, organizes the first company of **"medic"** instruction for members of the Hospital Corps at Fort Riley, Kansas.

1898

With the Spanish-American War looming, Congress passes a bill authorizing establishment of the **US Navy Hospital Corps**, signed into law by President William McKinley on June 17, 1898.

The **practicante**, an assistant to a physician, is introduced into Puerto Rico. (The role is abolished in 1931.)

1925

Mary Breckinridge establishes the **Frontier Nursing Service** in the mountains of Kentucky and builds Wendover, now a National Historic Landmark, marking the first effort to professionalize midwifery in the United States.

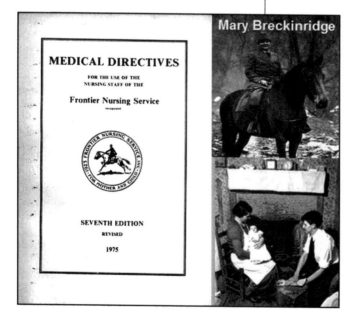

MEDICAL DIRECTIVES

FOR THE USE OF THE
NURSING STAFF OF THE

Frontier Nursing Service

SEVENTH EDITION

REVISED

1975

Mary Breckinridge

Founded by Mary Breckinridge, Frontier Nurses have been providing care in rural Kentucky for almost 90 years.

1930

Charles Higgins, MD, hires and trains Eddie Rogers to be his "medic" in urology at the Cleveland Clinic. As Higgins' assistant, Rogers becomes adept at providing therapeutic procedures to treat urological problems.

A young African American, **Vivien Theodore Thomas**, secures a job as surgical research technician with **Alfred Blalock, MD**, at Vanderbilt University, and in the 1940s helps to develop the procedures used to treat "blue baby syndrome." Although informally trained by Dr. Blalock, he becomes a pioneer in, and eventually a teacher of, cardiac surgical technique with Dr. Blalock at Johns Hopkins University. Although he has received no formal education, and has never personally treated a patient, he is awarded an honorary doctorate degree from the University in 1976.

Beginning in 1930, former military corpsmen receive on-the-job training from the **Federal Prison System** to extend the services of prison physicians. This eventually leads to the establishment of a **US Public Health Service PA Program** in July 1968 at the Medical Center for Federal Prisoners in Springfield, MO. The program is the

Community Health Aides are deployed to native villages in Alaska, often transported by helicopter.

AMOS N. JOHNSON, MD AND HENRY LEE "BUDDY" TREADWELL

Amos Johnson was a truly legendary general practitioner in rural North Carolina. In 1940 he hired and personally trained Buddy Treadwell, a young farm boy, to be a "doctor's assistant." As Buddy's skills grew, and Johnson became involved in state and national medical organizations, he increasingly left his practice and his patients in Buddy's care while he was away. Moreover, as Johnson became the leading figure in the transition of general practice to the specialty of Family Medicine, he openly credited Treadwell's competence to his own ability to participate in national affairs. He became the founding President of the new American Board of Family Medicine.

Johnson and Treadwell, and their symbiotic relationship, were well known and respected by the Duke University medical faculty. When Eugene Stead created the first PA program at Duke University, he often cited the Johnson/ Treadwell relationship as the model for the concept.

When Dr. Johnson died in 1975, the 25 year partnership came to an end. Although Treadwell was eligible, as an "informally trained" PA, to take the NCCPA examination, he declined, electing to return to the family business in rural Garland, North Carolina.

first to be federally sponsored, but was never accredited, and was phased out in the 1970s when PA training became widely available elsewhere.

1940

Community Health Aides are introduced in Alaska to improve the village health status of Eskimos and other Native Americans. Public Health Nurses are employed by the Territorial Department of Health to instruct village midwives.

Amos N. Johnson, MD, employs Henry "Buddy" Treadwell as a technician and, over time, trains him as a "doctor's assistant" to work in his rural general practice in Garland, NC. Johnson becomes a major participant in national medical organizations, frequently leaving Treadwell to care for his patients. The relationship becomes widely known, and accepted, throughout North Carolina.

EUGENE A. STEAD, JR., MD

Eugene A. Stead, Jr. is generally acknowledged as the leading educator of physicians during the last half of the 20th century. As Chair of Medicine at Duke University for 20 years following World War II, he mentored scores of students and faculty who became prominent scientists and academic leaders elsewhere. He promoted clinical research within his department, and gave rise to the concept of medical specialty training during residency.

Perhaps his most important contribution, however, stemmed from his recognition that physicians were too burdened by the mundane aspects of practice to further their learning. Observing how ex-military corpsmen were being used by specialty units at Duke, he conceived how useful they might be – with additional training – in the general practice of medicine. He announced his intention to begin a program in 1965 to train corpsmen as "physician's assistants." Started with four students, the program gained wide national attention, and became the model for a new health occupation that exploded across the country over the next few years. He counseled early on that the PA should always remain dependent, serving to extend the reach and scope of medical practice. Under those conditions, the potential for their ability to diagnose and treat, and to perform procedures, was unlimited.

Dr. Stead is considered to be the "father" of the PA profession. National PA Day is celebrated each year on his birthday, October 6. He died in 2005 at the age of 96.

1942

During World War II, **Eugene A. Stead, Jr, MD**, develops a fast track, 3-year medical curriculum to educate physicians at Emory University for military service. Without residents, he uses medical students to help staff **Emory University and Grady Hospitals in Atlanta, GA**. The experience provides a model for the competency-based medical curriculum developed to educate physician's assistants at Duke University in 1965.

The **Maritime Service** begins a **Hospital Corps School** at the Sheepshead Bay training station with surgeon, S.S. Heilwell, MD of the US Public Health Service in charge. This program is combined with the existing **Junior Assistant Purser School** in order to train a more skilled individual to serve on merchant marine ships during World War II. By 1944 more than 600 pursers had completed the advanced training.

1948

The United Nations establishes the World Health Organization.

1957-1970

The Formative Years

As specialization in medical practice grew following World War II, a growing shortage in primary care health manpower has become clear. At Duke University in 1957, the nation's foremost chair of medicine, and a visionary nurse begin a program to train nurses to provide direct assistance to physicians with emphasis on primary care. Having failed accreditation by the National League for Nursing (NLN), the program was discontinued, but the experience was not forgotten. In an address to the House of Delegates in 1960, an emerging leader of the AMA proposes the training of former military corpsmen as assistants to physicians. In 1965, Duke University establishes such a program with four ex-Navy corpsmen, creating a sensation in the national press. Within four years four other prototypes emerge. The Duke PA and University of Washington MEDEX programs are quickly emulated by other academic medical colleges. Meanwhile, the shortage of generalist physicians is compounded by the creation of Medicare and Medicaid, opening access to health services by millions of new patients. Two national commissions address the issue, promoting expansion of all efforts to support generalist physicians. By the end of the 1960s, the AMA formally endorses the concept of the "physician's assistant," and begins to explore accreditation of programs in order to achieve a common standard of training. The existing academic programs form a "registry" to assure the public of the qualifications of their graduates. Formalization of these processes will require compromise and cooperation, and is to be achieved in the next decade.

1957

Thelma Ingles, RN, begins a clinical sabbatical year with Dr. Stead, at Duke University, which leads to the establishment of a master's degree program for nurse clinicians at the School of Nursing. The program, funded by the Rockefeller Foundation, produces highly trained nurses who are taught primarily by physicians at Duke. Although highly successful, the program is denied accreditation by the National League for Nursing (NLN) because of the heavy reliance on physicians in the training program, and because Ms. Ingles lacked a degree in nursing. (She had a baccalaureate degree in English from UCLA, and had graduated from the prestigious nursing program at the Massachusetts General Hospital.) It is generally conceded that, had this innovative program been accredited, Stead would not have initiated the Duke University PA program with former

THELMA M. INGLES, RN, MA

Thelma Ingles is acknowledged as one of the leading nurse educators of the 20th century. Having obtained a baccalaureate degree in English literature from UCLA, and an MS from Case Western Reserve University, Ms. Ingles attended the rigorous hospital nursing program at the Massachusetts General Hospital. She was Chair of the Department of Medical-Surgical Nursing at Duke University when she took a sabbatical in 1958 to work with Eugene A. Stead to develop a program in advanced nursing, teaching nurses to assist physicians in their offices and at the bedside. Funded by the Rockefeller Foundation, the program led to a Master's degree as a clinical nurse specialist. The training was denied accreditation by the National League for Nursing, however, on the grounds that the nurses had been trained by physicians rather than nurses, and that Ms. Ingles did not possess a degree in nursing.

Ingles joined the Rockefeller Foundation in 1961, and began a career in nursing education that spanned the globe. Over the years she visited 52 countries. She was active in helping to improve nursing education in South America, establishing both BS and Masters' programs in Cali, Colombia. She was a consultant to schools of nursing in Turkey, Thailand, Russia, and Finland. She worked with the World Health Organization and the Peace Corps. She helped establish some of the first hospices in the United States.

It is ironic that the failed program she helped lead at Duke University provided a stimulus for the concept of the nurse practitioner which began in the decade of the 1960s, alongside the physician assistant profession.

military corpsmen eight years later. The PA profession might never have existed.

1959

US Surgeon General Leroy E. Burney, identifies a national shortage of medically trained personnel to provide basic medical services.

1961

An address to the House of Delegates of the AMA by newly elected Trustee, **Charles Hudson, MD**, is published in the *Journal of the American Medical Association*. Entitled, "Expansion of Medical Professional Services with Nonprofessional Personnel," it calls for a **"mid-level" provider** from the ranks of former military corpsmen. Movement toward the concept of the physician assistant is set in motion.

The World Health Organization (WHO) begins introducing and promoting new categories of health care workers in developing countries (e.g., Me'decin Africain, Dresser, Assistant Medical Officer, and Rural Health Technician).

CHARLES L. HUDSON, MD

The House of Delegates of the AMA was electrified in late 1960 by an address from Charles L. Hudson, a newly elected member of the Board of Trustees, who proposed that non-physicians be trained to assist doctors in providing health services. He cited precedent that he understood well, having served as a lieutenant colonel in the US Army in World War II, directing medical units in Southern Europe. His proposal gained wide support when it was published in JAMA in April, 1961. He rose through the ranks to become President Elect of the AMA in 1965, the year the first PA Program was begun at Duke University.

Having graduated from the University of Michigan, Dr. Hudson served his residency at University Hospitals, and spent his entire career with the Cleveland Clinic and Case Western Reserve University. He served on the board of the National Association of Blue Shield Plans, and was elected to the presidency of the Ohio State Medical Association. Dr. Hudson's presidency of the AMA proved to be challenging when Medicare and Medicaid were implemented in 1966, but he worked successfully to gain its acceptance by physicians.

Honoring his strong support of physician assistants, the Ohio Academy created an award in his name. He was elected an Honorary Member by the AAPA. Upon his death in 1992, he was buried with an AAPA lapel pin on his suit.

Hu C. Myers, MD

A unique approach to the training of physician assistants was created by Hu Myers. Born and raised in West Virginia, Dr. Myers received his medical training at Emory University in Georgia. An accomplished surgeon, he returned to West Virginia where, together with his father and brother, he established the Myers Clinic Hospital in Philippi, near Alderson Broadus College. He was instrumental in establishing a baccalaureate program in nursing at the college – the first degree-granting nursing program in the state.

After working to develop several allied health training programs at the hospital, his rural roots in a physician shortage area led him to conceive the concept of training assistants to physicians who would be cultured to remain in the state. Stimulated by Charles Hudson's address to the AMA in 1960, he first approached the administration of the college with the idea in 1963. His intent was to recruit high school graduates from the state into a baccalaureate program, the final two years of which would provide training in the art and science of medical practice. It was initially rejected by the Trustees, but following the establishment of Eugene Stead's widely publicized program at Duke University, was accepted by the College in 1967. It became the model for PA programs in small colleges with instruction provided by community physicians.

His book, *The Physician's Assistant: A Baccalaureate Curriculum* is a classic in the field.

1963

Hu Myers, MD, approaches the Alderson-Broaddus College Board of Trustees in Philippi, WV, about starting a four year degree-granting program to educate physician assistants similar to the degree granting nursing program that he had helped establish at the College in 1945. The Board turns him down.

1964

The Civil Rights Act is enacted as a landmark piece of legislation in the United States. The Act outlaws major forms of discrimination against African Americans, including racial segregation. It removes socioeconomic barriers to voter registration and ends racial segregation in schools, at the workplace and by facilities that serve the general public such as restaurants, bathrooms, hospitals and clinics.

Eugene A. Stead, Jr., MD, disillusioned by organized nursing's rejection of the advanced nurse clinician program that he and nurse educator, **Thelma Ingles**, had developed, announces in **a letter** to

April 21, 1964

Mr. Charles H. Frenzel
Duke Hospital

Dear Mr. Frenzel:

During the next ten years I would like to have a hand in training men to be physicians' assistants. This career would be open to men with a high-school or junior-college degree, or to anyperson who was sponsored by a physician because of work already performed in a hospital, physician's office, or laboratory. The physician's assistant would have one year of training in a physician-directed area in the Medical Center and one year of experience in a community hospital. He would be licensed by an appropriate change in the Medical Practice Act.

The physician's assistant would be able to differentiate in many ways. He could, under the doctor's direction, make home calls and see patients in the office. The physician would be responsible for determining the extent of his duties. In the hospital setting, he could be responsible for drawing blood, giving infusions, administering oxygen, performing bladder catheterizations, and giving emergency resuscitation. He would perform most of the straight service functions not done by medical students and interns.

In many instances, the physician assistant would, under the direction of the physician, form health care units which would operate in both the office and the home, as well as in the hospital. These units would care for all the acutely-ill patients and would consist of varying proportions of maids, aides, practical and graduate nurses.

The present structure of the Department of Medicine offers a good base for a start in this program. We have three laboratories (renal, cardiac and pulmonary) which have the necessary quota of physicians, professional nurses and sick patients. In the beginning we would like to concentrate on persons who have had some preliminary training in either the military service or VA hospitals. We would like to work out a program with the vocational training agency for one year of preliminary instruction at the high-school level.

I request that you call a meeting of the appropriate administrative personnel to discuss this program.

Sincerely,

Eugene A. Stead, Jr., M.D.

Carbon copy of a 1964 letter from Eugene A. Stead, Jr. to Duke University Hospital Administration, announcing his intention to initiate a physician assistant training program in 1965.

Duke Hospital Administrator, Charles H. Frenzel, his intention to develop a program for the "physician's assistant," using former military corpsmen, modeled after the relationship between **Amos N. Johnson, MD**, and **Henry Lee "Buddy" Treadwell**, his assistant, that was well known in the North Carolina community.

1965

As announced by Stead, the nation's first "physician assistant" educational program is inaugurated at Duke University. The Program accepts four **former Navy medical corpsmen**.

A *Reader's Digest* article about jobs in the health care industry mentions the development of the PA program at Duke University, causing a flood of inquiries from ex-military corpsmen.

A **White House Conference on Health** discusses the use of former military corpsmen/medics as "assistant medical officers."

Henry K. Silver, MD, and nurse educator **Loretta Ford** establish a four

HENRY K. SILVER, MD

Educated in California, Dr. Henry Silver arrived at the University of Colorado in 1957 as Vice Chair of the Department of Pediatrics. In 1965, together with Loretta C. Ford, EdD, he created a pediatric nurse practitioner program, a joint effort of the schools of medicine and nursing. It became the first successful NP program in the nation, and is considered today to be the model for the development of the NP profession. In 1968 he launched the Child Health Associate Program, designed for persons with two to three years of college to become physician assistants, providing primary care services to children. Among other distinctions, it became the first PA program to offer the Master's degree. Silver and his colleagues were diligent in documenting the competence, efficiency, and effectiveness of the practicing physician assistant.

In addition to his contributions to these new professions, Dr. Silver was a pioneer in child growth and development. The "Silver Syndrome," a failure of an infant to grow, bears his name. He was an early contributor to the recognition and management of child abuse and neglect. Having published more than 100 scientific articles, he was the longtime editor of the *Handbook of Pediatrics*, and of Current Pediatric Diagnosis and Treatment. He was a recipient of the prestigious Gustav O. Lienhard Award by the Institute of Medicine for outstanding achievement in improving health and services in the United States.

month Pediatric Nurse Practitioner program at the University of Colorado.

Medicare and Medicaid are passed by the United States Congress, expanding the need for basic medical services – already in short supply. The legislation stipulates that no reimbursement will be provided to segregated hospitals. The reorganization of US hospitals sets the stage for the development of new roles within hospital systems.

Richard Smith, MD, who later becomes the founder of the MEDEX Programs, is appointed by President Lyndon Johnson to lead the federal effort to desegregate the US hospital system.

Mao Zedong, Premier of China, calls for the training of **Barefoot Doctors** to provide basic medical services to rural Chinese populations. By 1968, the barefoot doctors program becomes integrated into national policy to establish "rural cooperative medical systems" (RCMS) throughout China. (The barefoot doctor system ends in 1981, when the agricultural communes are abolished.)

RICHARD A. SMITH, MD, MPH

With a medical degree from Howard University and an MPH from Columbia University, Dr. Richard Smith committed himself to a career that would bring health services to underserved populations in both the United States, and in developing countries. Two years with the Public Health Service on the Navajo Reservation in Arizona was followed by two years with the Peace Corps in Nigeria. After spending time in the Surgeon General's office, focusing on international health, he relocated to the University of Washington, where he developed the MEDEX concept in 1968.

An alternative to the Duke University model, the program in Seattle drew upon former career military corpsmen. Following only three months of formal instruction, the students were paired with rural practitioners in four western states, where they were expected to remain following graduation. He then helped replicate the MEDEX model in eight other medical colleges, and, with colleagues, formed the Council of MEDEX Programs. Although these prototype programs ultimately recruited outside the military ranks, and expanded the biomedical science component of their curriculum to meet accreditation standards, they retained their focus on assistants to physicians providing care to underserved populations.

Since 1972, Dr. Smith has been Director of the "MEDEX Group" and Professor at the University of Hawaii. Dr. Smith is a member of the Institute of Medicine, and of two international committees of the World Health Association.

1966

The **Willard Commission**, appointed by the AMA, recommends that the "general practice" of medicine be transformed into the specialty of **"family medicine"**, that a three year residency be required, and that a board be established to oversee formal certification.

The **Millis Commission** (Citizens Commission on Graduate Medical Education) reinforces creation of family medicine as a specialty, and defines the term **"primary care"** to mean first contact, management of common illness, and health maintenance. Such care is expected to be provided by general internists, general pediatricians, and family physicians. It is identified as the Nation's most critical health manpower issue.

A *Look Magazine* article entitled "More Than a Nurse; Less Than a Doctor" creates a sensation when it catapults the PA concept to national attention, but undermines attempts to foster nurses' acceptance of PAs.

Former military corpsmen are increasingly being informally trained to assist physicians in a variety of specialties and practice settings. National attention is brought to the issue in **People v Whittaker**, a case in which the State of California charged ex-Navy operating room technician, **Roger Whittaker**, an assistant to neurosurgeon, Dr. George

Stevenson, with "engaging in the unlicensed practice of medicine." While found guilty, both men were assessed only a small fine. Whittaker was invited by Eugene Stead to join the incoming class of students at Duke University. The case underscores a need for legislation to permit physicians to delegate tasks to qualified non-physicians.

1967

John W. Kirklin, MD, initiates the first **surgeon's assistant program** at the University of Alabama in Birmingham, AL.

The **first class** of three PAs, **Victor H. Germino**, **Kenneth F. Ferrell** and **Richard J. Scheele**, graduates from Duke University on October 6th.

Defendants George Stevenson and Roger Whittaker during trial in "People v Whittaker" in California in 1966.

JOHN W. KIRKLIN, MD

A graduate of Harvard Medical School, John Kirklin received his surgical training at the Mayo Clinic. Following service in World War II, he returned to the Mayo Clinic to become Chief of the Department of Surgery and a nationally prominent cardiac surgeon. Among his accomplishments, he developed a clinically workable heart-lung bypass machine that helped the Mayo Clinic to assume national leadership in surgery for valvular heart disease.

In 1966 he moved to the University of Alabama to become Chair of Surgery. From his experience with corpsmen during the war, he knew that much of the work of a surgeon could be done equally well by well-trained assistants. Following the experiment at Duke University, he and his wife, Margaret Kirklin, MD, proceeded to create the first training program for surgeons' assistants. Margaret served as the Academic Director. Working with the American College of Surgeons, he helped to develop a statement of "Educational Essentials," and persuaded the AMA to expand its program of accreditation of physician assistants to include trained assistants in surgery.

Dr. Kirklin was the longtime editor of the *Journal of Thoracic and Cardiovascular Surgery*, and the author of a two volume textbook of cardiac surgery that was continued into subsequent editions, long after his retirement, by residents he had trained. He died following a head injury in 2004.

1968

Hu C. Myers, MD, again approaches the Trustees, and this time receives approval to establish the **first baccalaureate degree program for PAs** at Alderson-Broaddus College in Philippi, WV.

Duke University hosts the **first of four national conferences on physician assistants** to explore the issues of development and standardization of educational program curricula, study and promotion of the PA concept to professional, private and Federal organizations, and the development of model legislation for PAs.

The **American Association of Physician's Assistants (AAPA)** is established by Duke University PA students and alumni, and is incorporated in NC. Its stated purposes are to encourage its members to render honest, loyal and efficient service to the medical profession, and quality care to the public whom they serve. **William (Bill) Stanhope, PA**, is elected as the first President.

Certificate signing, October 6, 1967. Medical School Dean William Anlyan signs certificates of the first three Duke University PA graduates. The date is coincidentally Dr. Stead's birthday and becomes celebrated as "PA Day."

1969

Richard Smith, MD, launches the MEDEX Program at the University of Washington, Seattle WA in partnership with the Washington State Medical Association. It is designed to rapidly deploy ex-military corpsmen to rural primary care practices throughout the Northwest.

The American Hospital Association and the Joint Commission on Accreditation of Hospitals release a report on the "Utilization of Physician's Assistants in the Hospital."

At the request of the Assistant Secretary of Health, Roger O. Egeberg, Alfred M. Sadler, Jr., MD, and Blair L. Sadler, JD, of the National Institutes of Health (NIH) complete an intensive nationwide survey of all licensed allied health occupations. Their report recommends that State Medical Practice Acts be amended to permit the practice of physician assistants under the supervision

WILLIAM D. STANHOPE, MS, PA

In April of 1968, during the fourth year of the existence of the Duke University PA program, the students and recent graduates of the program gathered in the hospital GI laboratory to form the American Association of Physician's Assistants (later, the Academy). Although a second year student, William Stanhope was elected the first President. He served two terms, and, later, two years as Secretary, working to recruit membership from students and graduates of other emerging programs, and establishing the AAPA as the voice of the new profession.

Following graduation, and after a year at Alderson Broadus College, Stanhope was asked to establish a PA program at the University of Oklahoma, where he became the first PA to direct a program, and the first to hold a tenured faculty position at an American medical college. He recruited several of his former Duke classmates – two of whom later served as presidents of AAPA.

Active on the national scene, Stanhope served on the advisory committee to the NBME that helped to develop the first certifying examination for PAs, and was a participant in the formation of the NCCPA in 1974. In 1978, he became the first PA to be selected as a Robert Wood Johnson Health Policy Fellow. He was subsequently involved in PA education at several other programs, while maintaining an active orthopedic PA practice.

Stanhope currently serves as a Trustee of the Physician Assistant History Society.

of a physician as long as both the PA and MD are responsible for these activities.

1970

Kaiser Permanente becomes the first HMO to employ PAs.

A consortium of PA programs establishes the **American Registry of Physicians' Associates (ARPA)**. It is incorporated in NC to grant and issue certificates to graduates of approved programs, or others who can "demonstrate by examination" that they possess the knowledge and skills of a graduate of an approved program.

Henry K. Silver, MD, establishes the **Child Health Associate (CHA) Program** at the University of Colorado (a PA Program with emphasis on Pediatrics).

The American Medical Association (AMA) Council on Health Manpower endorses the PA concept. The House of Delegates adopts **"Guidelines for the Development of New Health Occupations."**

With the recognition that more than 100 programs throughout the country have arisen to train what are termed "physician's assistants," and that they vary widely in length and depth of training, and in quality of instruction, the Board of Medicine of the **National Academy of Sciences** releases a report classifying physician's assistants as Types A, B, or C. **Type A** assistants are broadly trained in an academic institution, across the full range of specialties, in a program of at least two years in length. **Type B** assistants are narrowly, but intensively, trained in a particular specialty. **Type C** assistants are broadly trained, but in less depth over a shorter length of time. National medical organizations respond by making it clear that their focus will be on the "Type A" assistant to the primary care physician.

Martha Ballenger releases a report of a project, conducted at Duke University, on **"model legislation"** for physician assistant practice. In California, Governor Ronald Reagan signs Assembly Bill 2109 into law on September 17, 1970. It directs the Board of Medical Examiners to establish this new category of health professional. Thus, **California** becomes the first state to enact **enabling legislation** for physician assistants.

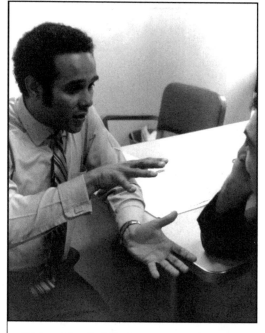

Richard Smith, MD, founder of the MEDEX model of PA training, pioneered in providing primary care services to rural populations where physicians were in short supply.

1971-1980

Establishing a Profession

The structure of a profession rests upon four pillars: A society of practitioners; an association of educational programs training those practitioners; a nationally recognized body charged with accreditation of the programs; and a process of certification of graduates in the public interest. By the middle of the decade of the 1970s all four of these entities are in place, and functioning with paid executive management. AAPA, established in 1968 by students and alumni of the Duke program, extends membership to graduates from programs around the country, and becomes the legitimate voice for the profession. APAP is formed in 1972 in order to share information among programs regarding curriculum and admission policy. Foundation funding in 1973 permits the establishment of a National Office to manage the affairs of both organizations. The several program models converge as the AMA, together with four medical specialty societies, begins the process of accreditation in 1972. The NBME administers an examination in 1973, followed by the formation, a year later, of the NCCPA, a consortium of societies and agencies, charged with oversight of the certification process. Federal funding, authorized under the 1971 Health Manpower Act, stimulates an explosion of training, tripling the number of programs in a single year, 1972. Begun as a Federal study, a foundation-funded book is published in 1972, tracing the origins of the PA concept, and suggesting policy direction for a new profession. Following four successful conferences, Duke University passes the baton of leadership to the new organizations to create, in 1973, the first nation-wide conference on "New Health Practitioners." States begin to adopt amendments to their medical practice acts which allow delegation of tasks by physicians to trained assistants. Multiple published studies conclude that PAs function at a level at least comparable to a control group of medical house officers. The AAPA establishes a House of Delegates to govern policy.

1971

The American Medical Association and the American Hospital Association recommend a moratorium on licensure of additional health occupations.

The **Comprehensive Health Manpower Training Act (PL92-157)** authorizes funding for physician assistant education and deployment.

The American Association of Physician Associates publishes its first official journal, ***Physician's Associate***.

Cartoonist Dick Moores introduces the general public to physician's assistants in his comic strip, *Gasoline Alley*, when **Chipper Wallet**, a leading character, becomes a PA.

The AMA House of Delegates adopts **"Essentials for an Educational Program for the Assistant to the Primary Care Physician."**

The first postgraduate residency program for PAs in surgery is established at the Montefiore Medical Center in Bronx, NY by **Marvin Gliedman, MD, Richard Rosen, MD**, and **Clara Vanderbilt, R-PA.**

1972

Upon recommendation of its Goals and Priorities Committee, the National Board of Medical Examiners approves **development of a certifying examination** for the assistant to the primary care physician. **Barbara J. Andrew, PhD,** is chosen to direct the project. **Edmund D. Pellegrino, MD**, is appointed by **John P. Hubbard, MD,** President of the NBME, to chair a Special Advisory Committee that includes representatives of the AMA.

The **Association of Physician Assistant Programs (APAP)** is established with sixteen charter members to facilitate communication and cooperation among physician assistant educational programs at universities and colleges throughout the United States. **Alfred M. Sadler, Jr., MD,** is elected as the organization's first president.

The first book written about PAs, ***The Physician's Assistant: Today and Tomorrow***, by **Alfred M. Sadler, Jr., MD, Blair L. Sadler, JD**, and **Ann. A. Bliss, RN, MSW,** is published by Yale University Press – based on a "White Paper" that was funded by the Carnegie

Gasoline Alley Comic Strip. Dick Moores (left), cartoonist. Image from article "Gasoline Alley shows Doc encouraging Chipper to become a PA." Appeared in March 12, 1971 issue of *The Intercom*, Duke University Medical Center.

Corporation, the Commonwealth Fund, the Foundation for the Aid to Crippled Children, the Macy Foundation and the Rockefeller Foundation.

The American Medical Association forms a **Joint Review Committee on Educational Programs for Assistants to the Primary Care Physician (JRC-PA)** to evaluate compliance with the "Essentials" adopted by the AMA House of Delegates. **Malcolm Peterson, MD**, of Johns Hopkins is elected the first Chairman. **Lawrence M. Detmer** is named Executive Secretary. Sponsoring

(Collaborating) Organizations include the American College of Physicians, the American Society of Internal Medicine, the American Academy of Family Physicians, the American Academy of Pediatrics and the Association of American Medical Colleges.

The Bureau of Health Professions Health Resources Administration awards its first contracts to support the development of primary care physician assistant educational programs.

JOHN P. HUBBARD, MD

Renowned pediatric cardiologist John P. Hubbard, an authority on the prevention and management of rheumatic fever, was recruited from Harvard in 1952 by the NBME to become its first fulltime executive. As President of the Board he directed the transition from traditional essay examination to the vastly more reliable and cost-effective multiple choice testing. He expanded the reach of the NBME by developing examinations that states could use in lieu of their own testing, and that the ECFMG could rely upon for the certification of foreign medical graduates.

In 1971 the NBME established an ad-hoc committee to evaluate other avenues for its activity. A major outcome was the development by the Board of an examination for the "assistant to the primary care physician" - the first involvement by the NBME in examining candidates other than physicians. Hubbard appointed an advisory committee of PA educational leaders, and recruited Barbara J. Andrew, PhD to direct the project. Together, they created a "role delineation study" to define the knowledge and tasks appropriate to the PA. The resulting certifying examination was first administered in December, 1973. Hubbard then worked with the AMA to establish the NCCPA, the organization responsible for PA certification today.

Dr. Hubbard retired as President of the NBME in 1974. He died in 1990.

Nine sponsoring U.S. colleges of medicine establish a **National Council of MEDEX Programs** to advance the cause of rural health care.

1973

A **First Annual Conference on New Health Practitioners** is held at Sheppard Air Force Base, Wichita Falls, TX with 275 attendees. Sponsored by APAP and AAPA, the Conference is a successor to the four annual Duke Conferences on Physician Assistants, and is open to nurse practitioners as well as PAs. The

Association of Physician Assistant Programs was established in 1972 with Alfred Sadler, MD, elected as the organization's first president.

ALFRED M. SADLER, JR., MD

While serving in the Public Health Service in the late 1960s, Dr. Sadler and his twin brother, Blair, a lawyer, studied the use of physician extenders in the practice of medicine. They visited the emerging physician assistant training programs, analyzed their impact and produced a report to the Secretary of DHEW recommending that state medical practice acts be amended to permit PAs to practice.

In 1970 Dr. Sadler joined the Yale University faculty, where he developed and directed a PA training program. With funding from five foundations, he wrote the seminal book on the PA concept, *The Physician's Assistant: Today and Tomorrow* (coauthored by Blair Sadler and Ann Bliss).

In 1972 he was elected the founding President of APAP, and with Dr. Piemme planned the first annual PA conference (1973). Together they raised foundation funds to establish a National Office for APAP and the AAPA. Dr. Sadler worked closely with the AMA to establish PA program accreditation, and with the NBME to create the first PA certifying examination.

Dr. Sadler joined the Robert Wood Johnson Foundation in 1973, where he advocated for the PA profession. After years in private practice, working with PAs and NPs, he was asked to serve as a Trustee of the PA History Society in 2009. He now serves as President Elect.

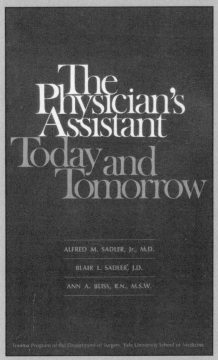

Sadler, Sadler & Bliss Book Cover. The Physician's Assistant: Today and Tomorrow. Published by Carl Purington Rollins Printing-Office of Yale University Press, 1972.

meeting becomes recognized as the first of the annual conferences of AAPA.

Alfred M. Sadler, Jr., MD, and **Thomas E. Piemme, MD**, receive funding from three foundations in New York – an amount matched by the Robert Wood Johnson Foundation – to establish a National Office in Washington, DC to

ANN A. BLISS, RN, MSW

As both a nurse and a mental health social worker, Ann Bliss served as Head Nurse at Yale-New Haven Hospital when the PA Program was established at Yale University in 1971. With strong beliefs in an interdependent team model of medical care, she was a maverick among nurses, but a perfect fit for the emerging PA profession.

Ms. Bliss coauthored the landmark book, *The Physician's Assistant: Today and Tomorrow*, with Alfred and Blair Sadler in 1972, contributing her insightful views of the history of nursing, and shared responsibility for the patient. She served the Yale PA program in the admissions process, and taught personality development and psychopathology to students for 25 years.

With a background in medical writing, she became the Managing Editor of the *PA Journal* during its formative years. In 1977 she co-edited a compendium of studies entitled, *The New Health Professionals: Nurse Practitioners and Physician's Assistants*. She served as a Yale-based member of the staff of the Robert Wood Johnson Foundation, promoting the funding of joint PA-NP training, and expanded roles for nurses in primary care and emergency medicine.

Ann Bliss retired from the Yale University Medical Faculty in 1996. She continues, however, her private practice of psychotherapy. In 2011, she became a Trustee of the PA History Society.

serve both AAPA and APAP with a full time staff.

The American Medical Association convenes a meeting of a number of medical professional organizations and government agencies to explore the feasibility of a "Commission" to govern the process of certification of physician assistants.

The American College of Surgeons (ACS) becomes a sponsoring organization of the JRC-PA and publishes *Essentials of an Approved Educational Program for the Surgeon's Assistant*.

The National Board of Medical Examiners (NBME) administers the first **Certifying Examination** for Assistants to the Primary Care Physician to 880 candidates, 10% of whom are graduates of nurse practitioner programs. The exam consists of multiple-choice questions and patient management problems using invisible ink technology to expose pertinent information.

LAWRENCE M. (MAC) DETMER

Born, raised and educated in Kansas, Mac Detmer studied hospital administration at the University of Minnesota. Following several years as an administrator at Johns Hopkins, he joined the staff of the American Hospital Association when training programs for allied health occupations were transitioning from their traditional hospital base to community colleges. With that background, he was recruited in 1971 by the American Medical Association to serve as the executive for the newly created Joint Review Committee on Educational Programs for Physician Assistants, a joint accreditation venture of the AMA and four medical specialty societies.

Detmer guided the JRC-PA for 20 years. During that time he worked closely with AAPA and APAP to gain recognition, and eventually representation, in 1974 and 1978, respectively. He organized workshops to train clinicians and educators, both physicians and PAs, to be site visitors, and developed a self-study guide for programs to use in preparation for accreditation review. He later supported a name change to the Accreditation Review Committee (ARC-PA), now an independent accrediting body headquartered in Atlanta GA.

Following his work with the physician assistant profession, Detmer went on to head accreditation for all of the allied health professions for the AMA. He retired in 1998, and lives in Evanston IL.

A highly influential Conference which addressed important policy issues for the emerging field of mid-level practitioners is sponsored by the Macy Foundation of New York. The results are published as a book entitled: *Intermediate-Level Health Practitioners*, edited by Lippard and Purcell for the Josiah Macy, Jr. Foundation.

Harold Sox, MD, and **Richard Tompkins, MD,** publish a landmark paper in the *New England Journal of Medicine* (288:818-24) entitled "The Training of Physician's Assistants: The Use of the Clinical Algorithm System for Patient Care, Audit of Performance and Education."

1974

AAPA becomes a full participating member of the Joint Review Committee on Educational Programs for PAs (JRC-PA). The Committee reviews physician assistant and surgeon assistant programs and makes recommendations to the Committee on Allied Health Education and Accreditation (CAHEA) of the AMA.

THOMAS E. PIEMME, MD

A graduate of the University of Pittsburgh, Dr. Thomas E. Piemme arrived at the George Washington University in 1970 as Professor of Medicine, responsible for ambulatory medical services. In 1972 he developed a PA training program to meet the primary care needs of the clinic population. He was present at the last of the Duke Conferences, when APAP was formed, serving as the second President, following the Founding President, Dr. Alfred M. Sadler, Jr.

Together, Drs. Sadler and Piemme initiated planning for the first Annual Conference on New Health Practitioners (now the annual meeting of AAPA), held in 1973, and raised foundation support for a National Office in Washington, DC, to serve both AAPA and APAP.

Active with the National Board of Medical Examiners, Dr. Piemme was instrumental in persuading the NBME to create a certifying examination for PAs. When the NCCPA was formed to assume responsibility for eligibility and standards for the examination, he became its first President. As Chair of the Primary Care Task Force of the Association of American Medical Colleges, Dr. Piemme brought physician assistants into the national dialog on priorities for medical education.

Dr. Piemme was asked in 2009 to become a Trustee of the Physician Assistant History Society. He became its President in 2012.

The **AAPA and APAP joint national office** opens in Washington, DC. **Donald W. Fisher, PhD**, serves as the first executive director.

Fourteen National health organizations come together to form the **National Commission on Certification of Physician's Assistants (NCCPA)** to provide oversight regarding eligibility and standards for the NBME examination, and to assure state medical boards, employers, and the public of the competency of PAs. **Thomas E. Piemme, MD**, is elected the first President. **David L. Glazer** is selected as the first Executive Director. An office is opened in December in Atlanta, GA.

The NCCPA and the NBME introduce reliable observational checklists into the PA certification examination in order to assess the candidate's ability to perform a physical examination. It is the first medical professional examination to do so.

The Association of American Medical Colleges (AAMC) holds a two and a half day Institute on Primary Care in Chicago, chaired by **Thomas E. Piemme, MD**, and **Steven A. Schroeder, MD**. A half-day session on "New Health Practitioners" is

DONALD W. FISHER, PHD

With a doctorate in anatomy, Donald W. Fisher was teaching basic science and directing the PA Program at the University of Mississippi when he was tapped to become the Executive Director of the new National Office for both AAPA and APAP in 1973. Accreditation and certification were in their infancy. Fisher was instrumental, in 1974, in obtaining adequate representation for AAPA in the new NCCPA, and in the Joint Review Committee on Accreditation of PAs. He traveled extensively throughout the country to help AAPA constituent chapters gain or improve PA enabling legislation.

When he began his tenure, AAPA had 1568 members – most of whom were students; APAP had 24 member programs; only a handful of states had adequate legislation. By the time he left in 1980, the profession had seen explosive growth. AAPA membership had grown fourfold; APAP member programs had doubled; 45 states had incorporated amendments into their medical practice acts.

Meanwhile both organizations had enhanced the quality of their research, publications, and membership services. The inaugural PA conference in 1973 had become the annual meeting of the AAPA. It had adopted a House of Delegates. Hours of continuing education, and the numbers of attendees and exhibitors at the meetings had grown exponentially.

Since leaving AAPA, Dr. Fisher has been President and CEO of the American Medical Group Association.

chaired by **Alfred M. Sadler, Jr., MD**. The session helps to incorporate the training of non-physicians into medical education.

Construction of the Trans-Alaska Pipeline from Prudhoe to Valdez begins. Physician assistants are chosen to provide medical services to the more than 10,000 workers employed on the project.

The Robert Wood Johnson Foundation funds the collaborative training of PAs and NPs at several major medical centers.

Komaroff and colleagues publish "Protocols for Physician Assistants" in the *New England Journal of Medicine* (290; 307-312).

1975

An updated and expanded version of the Sadler, Sadler, and Bliss book entitled *The Physician's Assistant Today and Tomorrow: Issues Confronting New Health Practitioners* is published by Ballinger Press. It contains the most authoritative history, bibliography, and

DAVID L. GLAZER, MS

Shortly following its formation in August, 1974, the NCCPA chose David Glazer, Associate Director of the PA Program at Emory University, as its first Executive Director. A psychologist with a background in testing and measurement, Glazer assumed the responsibility for eligibility, standard setting, and test administration from the NBME, which had created the PA certifying examination in 1973.

Critical to the mission of the NCCPA and its 14 component societies, was a system of maintenance of certification by periodic reregistration through demonstrated continuing medical education, and recertification by examination. Within months of beginning work, the staff of the Commission had issued certificates to those who had taken the examination in 1973 and 1974, and begun the work of tracking hours of AAPA-approved CME.

Glazer traveled extensively to promote recognition of the examination by the states. Within two years, 33 states adopted regulations requiring a currently valid NCCPA certificate for practice; within a decade, the requirement was universal. As the roles and responsibilities of PAs became diversified, he guided test committees through an evolution of the scope of the examination. By 1980 the NCCPA examination process was recognized as the standard among allied health occupations.

After 20 years, Glazer left to become a regional Director for the American Medical Group Association.

policy recommendations to date, on the development of the profession. (Full text of the book is available without charge on the PAHx website.)

NCCPA issues its first certificates to PAs who passed the examinations administered by the National Board of Medical Examiners in 1973 and 1974. The clock begins running on reregistration of the certificate every two years, based on hours of continuing medical education, and recertification every six years, based upon reexamination. PAs begin using the designation PA-C to reflect that they have passed the examination, and been certified by the NCCPA. State medical boards quickly begin recognizing the certificate as a qualification for practice within the individual states.

1976

Federal support of PA education continues under grants from the **Health Professions Assistance Act (PL 94-484)**.

NATIONAL BOARD OF MEDICAL EXAMINERS
3930 CHESTNUT STREET, PHILADELPHIA, PA. 19104

Announcement of the

1973 Certifying Examination for Primary Care Physician's Assistants

Wednesday
December 12, 1973

NBME cover page of pamphlet announcing the 1973 Certifying Examination for PAs. National Board of Medical Examiners, Philadelphia, PA.

APAP receives a three-year grant from the Robert Wood Johnson Foundation that provides continued core staff support for the APAP/AAPA national office and establishes a research division.

A Joint Research and Review Committee of the AAPA/APAP designs and sends the first National PA Survey to 4,583 PAs of whom 83% report providing primarily primary care services.

1977

The New Health Professionals: Nurse Practitioners and Physician's Assistants, by **Ann Bliss, RN**, and **Eva Cohen**, is published by Aspen Systems Corp.

AAPA Education and Research Foundation (later renamed the Physician Assistant Foundation) is incorporated to obtain public and private funds to support student scholarships and research about the PA profession.

Rural Health Clinic Services Act (PL95-210) provides Medicare reimbursement for PA and nurse practitioner (NP) services in rural clinics.

Health Practitioner (later named *Physician Assistant*) journal begins publication and is distributed to PAs as the official publication of the AAPA.

1978

The Physician's Assistant: Innovation in the Medical Division of Labor, by **Eugene Schneller, PhD**, is published.

AAPA House of Delegates becomes the policy-making legislative body of the Academy. **William Hughes, PA-C**, is first Speaker of the House.

The **US Air Force** begins appointing PAs as **commissioned officers** establishing a precedent for the uniformed services.

1979

APAP becomes an official collaborating member of the JRC-PA. **E. Harvey Estes, Jr., MD, Linda K. Davies, PA-C,** and **Frances Horvath, MD**, are selected as the first three APAP representatives.

1980

The Graduate Medical Education National Advisory Committee (GMENAC) issues a report projecting an oversupply of physicians by year 2000 unless steps are taken to reduce the production of physicians. One of the recommendations is to integrate manpower planning of physicians and non-physician providers and support training of non-physician providers aimed at placing them into medical shortage areas.

The NCCPA provides an add-on **"Proficiency Examination in Surgery"** for PAs. Certification still depends upon passing the "core" PA National Certifying Examination (PANCE).

END OF THE DECADE

Number of programs **accredited: 42**

Number of physician assistants **certified: 9,431**

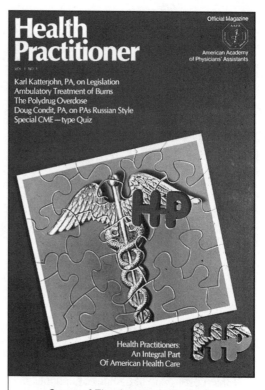

Official Magazine

Health Practitioner

VOL 1 NO 1

American Academy of Physicians' Assistants

Karl Katterjohn, PA, on Legislation
Ambulatory Treatment of Burns
The Polydrug Overdose
Doug Condit, PA, on PAs Russian Style
Special CME—type Quiz

Health Practitioners:
An Integral Part
Of American Health Care

Cover of First Issue of the *Health Practitioner* Magazine published by F&F Publications, New York, NY, May/June 1977.

ADDITIONAL PA LEADERS OF THE DECADE

JOHN A. BRAUN, PA, MPH

John A. Braun, a Navy hospital corpsman and graduate of the Duke University PA Program (1968), is a founding member and past president (1972) of the AAPA. He obtained his MPH from UNC-Chapel Hill in 1972; conducting the first task analysis of PA graduates. He was hired as Chief of the PA Staff at the Bureau of Health Manpower, NIH to administer the first federally funded authority for the establishment of PA programs; he was later assigned to DHEW Region IV as Chief of Primary Care Health Professions Staff, funding a variety of programs. He remained with the Bureau until 1980 administering over $72 Million in health professions educational program grants and contracts. In 1980 – 1992 he was President and CEO of MEMS, Inc., operating urgent care centers in NC and FL. For the next thirteen years he was a Clinical Research Associate and Global Clinical Trial Team Leader in the pharmaceutical industry.

E. CARL FASSER, PA

E. Carl Fasser, a former US Air Force corpsman and 1969 graduate of the Duke PA Program, is a founding member and twice president of the AAPA, an early NCCPA commissioner and a past president of the APAP (now PAEA). He participated in the formation of the NCCPA and the AMA's accreditation Joint Review Committee (JRC-PA), the AAPA House of Delegates and the AAPA Student Academy. In 1971, he helped establish the PA Program at the Baylor College of Medicine, Houston, TX and has spent most of his academic life there as its director. He is also the founding Dean of the School of Health Sciences and Chairman of the Department of PA Studies at the Massachusetts College of Pharmacy and Health Sciences in Boston. Fasser has received numerous awards, including the AAPA Founder's Award and the PAEA Master Faculty Award. His academic interests encompass interdisciplinary education and health services research.

THOMAS R. GODKINS, PA, MPH

Thomas R. Godkins, a Navy corpsman, graduated from the Duke PA Program in 1969. He is a founding member and twice president of the AAPA (1972-73 and 1975-1976). Godkins is the first non-physician president (1979-1980) of the APAP. He was the first PA employed by the Mayo Clinic in Rochester, MN and the first PA to be placed in a satellite clinic. As a pioneering member of the Oklahoma Academy of PAs, he helped gain PA enabling legislation for the state. He received a MPH from the University of Oklahoma and served on the faculty of the University's Health Sciences Center for 35 years; 10 years as Associate Director of the PA Program and 25 years as Assistant Provost, Director of Capital Planning, and Associate Vice President for Facilities Management. He died soon after retirement in 2010.

STEPHEN L. JOYNER, PA-C

Stephen L. Joyner is a former medical corpsman (US Air Force) and a 1968 graduate of the Duke University PA Program. Joyner is a founding member of the AAPA and of the North Carolina Academy of Physician Assistants serving on each organization's Board of Directors. He was a founding Commissioner of the NCCPA, and served as the first Treasurer. In 1982 he was named an Honorary Commissioner. Joyner entered family practice in 1969 in Ayden, N.C. forming one of the first single MD/PA teams in the country. In 1982 he became administrative director of the East Carolina University Transplant and Organ Procurement Program, and was instrumental in establishing the Carolina Organ Procurement Agency, now known as Carolina Donor Services. In 1989 he opened and co-owned Greenville Health Care Center, from which he retired in 2002.

GEORGE McCULLOUGH, PA-C

George McCullough, a US Air Force corpsman and pharmacist technician, graduated as a member of the second class of PAs from the joint Sheppard Air Force Base/University of Nebraska PA program in 1972. In 1974, he became the first enlisted (active duty) person to be elected to the AAPA Board of Directors. He was the first PA assigned to the Surgeon General's office to develop PA and NP performance regulations for the uniformed services. As a Washington insider, he was an active advocate for the commissioning of PAs in the US Air Force. When commissioning was approved, McCullough was serving as a PA on the White House medical staff; the first PA to be assigned to this post; and was the first US Air Force PA to be commissioned. The ceremony was held in 1978 at the White House during the Carter Administration.

JOYCE NICHOLS, PA-C

Joyce Nichols, the first woman to be formally educated as a PA, graduated from Duke in 1970. As the first African American woman PA she was a strong advocate for minorities in the Profession and served on the AAPA Board of Directors where she helped launch and also chaired the Minority Affairs Committee. She practiced in one of the first satellite clinics in rural North Carolina and then at Lincoln Health Center, a historically black community hospital and hospital in Durham. As a faculty member at Duke, she taught many medical and PA students. She was a staunch advocate for tenants' rights and served as a Commissioner for the Durham Housing Authority. In 1996 she received the AAPA's Paragon Award as "Humanitarian of the Year". She died at home in Durham in 2012.

STEPHEN TURNIPSEED, MPH, PA

A veteran of Special Forces Medical Counterinsurgancy in Vietnam, Steve Turnipseed entered the first class of the MEDEX Northwest Program, and became one of the first PAs to work at Group Health Cooperative in Seattle. He was the first MEDEX graduate to serve on the newly aligned Board of AAPA in 1973. He served as one of the first three PAs on the AMA's JRC-PA, and as one of the two PAs on the NBME Advisory Committee as it began developing the first examination – thus having a role in the inauguration of both accreditation and certification. He was active in the founding of the AAPA's Minority Affairs Committee in the 1970s. He helped to establish the PA Program at the Charles R. Drew University in Los Angeles, and was a consultant to emerging programs at North Dakota, Utah, Howard University, and Meharry Medical College.

CLARA E. VANDERBILT, PA-C

Clara E. Vanderbilt, a graduate of the Duke University PA Program (1971), was one of the first two PA surgical residents employed by Montefiore Medical Center, Bronx, NY. With Drs. Marvin Gleidman and Richard Rosen, Vanderbilt helped establish the first PA surgical postgraduate program in the country and served as its director from 1978 until she retired in 2000. She served on the AAPA Board of Directors from 1972 to 1975 and was the organization's vice president in 1975. Vanderbilt is a founding member and the first elected president of the New York State Society of PAs (1976). She was also one of the first PAs appointed to the NCCPA serving from 1977 to 1983, and was twice elected president of the Association of Postgraduate PA Programs. Vanderbilt received the AAPA presidential award in 1983 and the 20th anniversary award in 1988.

1981–1990

NATIONWIDE ADOPTION

The decade of the 1980s represents nationwide dissemination of an established profession. There is growing recognition of PA contributions to the medical workforce. With a single exception, all states now authorize the delegation of responsibility by the physician to the physician assistant, provided that tasks assigned are within the scope of practice of the physician. Revision of statutes allows prescriptive privileges in most states. There is a clear trend toward specialization with PAs employed by physicians practicing all specialties. By the end of the decade, branches of the military service begin to grant commissioned officer status to PAs. In 1981 the NCCPA introduces the process of recertification by examination. In 1986, reimbursement of PA services under Medicare, Part B, is authorized under the Omnibus Budget Reconciliation Act. The profession is poised for another period of rapid growth.

1981

Staffing Primary Care in 1990: Physician Replacement and Costs Savings, by Jane Cassels Record, reveals that PAs based in an HMO can provide 79% of care traditionally performed by primary care physicians at 50% of the cost.

APAP conducts a third national survey of students and graduates, with Robert Wood Johnson Foundation support. The results of the three national surveys are merged to establish a National PA Database. The AAPA assumes responsibility for updating and maintaining this database.

NCCPA introduces the **Physician Assistant National Recertification Examination (PANRE)**. PAs who fail the exam are recertified for two years, but are required to retake the examination within that time period.

1982

Physician Assistants: Their Contribution to Health Care, by **Henry Perry, MD**, and Bina Breitner, is published by Human Sciences Press.

1983

NCCPA's Physician Assistant National Certifying Examination (PANCE) is redesigned to include three com-

Announcement for the First PA Recertification Examination in 1981

ponents: a general knowledge core, an extended core in either surgery or primary care, and observational checklist clinical skills problems (CSPs).

1984

First Annual Report on Physician Assistant Educational Programs in the United States, by Denis Oliver, PhD, is published by the Association of Physician Assistant Programs (APAP).

Judith B. Willis, PA-C, is the first woman elected president of AAPA.

The Canadian National Forces begin training and using PAs.

JUDITH B. WILLIS, PA

In a profession that began with former military corpsmen, and remained male-dominated through the first decade, women were increasingly being admitted to training in the late 1970s. In 1984, Judy Willis became the first woman to serve as President of the AAPA. As a part of her rich career in administration, she later served the Academy as the first Director of Research from 1988 to 1994.

With an undergraduate degree in speech pathology from Indiana University, Ms. Willis attended the PA program at Western Michigan University. After post-graduate work in health policy, she became Director of Research and Education for the Southwestern Michigan Area Health Education Center. That was followed by appointment as Director of the Office of Research at the Health Care Financing Administration (HCFA) in the Department of Health and Human Services. She then became Deputy Director and Special Assistant for Drug Policy at the National Drug Policy Board, reporting directly to the Secretary of HHS, and to the Attorney General overseeing a budget of nearly $4 billion.

In 1994 Ms. Willis was the founder, and served as President and CEO, of CIVS, Inc., a national healthcare provider credentialing service, the largest company of its kind in the industry. After the company was acquired by CareData Inc., she joined the faculty at Kings College in Charlotte, NC where she teaches to the present day.

To honor her service to the profession, and her government and corporate leadership, Ms. Willis has received the Presidential Award for Leadership from the AAPA.

Alternatives in Health Care Delivery, edited by **Reginald Carter, PhD, PA**, and **Henry Perry, MD**, is published by Warren H. Green, Inc.

1985

AAPA's **Burroughs Wellcome Health Policy Fellowship** is created. **Marshal Sinback, PA-C**, becomes the first fellow.

AAPA and APAP initiate an important joint project providing PA graduates with a national job bank service: **PA JOB Find**.

NCCPA's Physician Assistant National Certifying Examination is open to informally trained professionals for the last time.

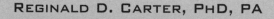

REGINALD D. CARTER, PhD, PA

Dr. Reginald Carter's long service to the PA profession dates from the early 1970s when he played a major role in research and development for the AAPA, leading the longitudinal studies of graduates of the early programs. He has served as President of PAEA, and is recognized as the founder of the Physician Assistant History Society.

A native of North Carolina, Carter received his baccalaureate and doctoral degrees from Wake Forest University. He was pursuing post-doctoral work, and teaching physiology at Duke University when he was asked to assume the role of associate director of the Duke PA program. Well-grounded in the basic sciences, he became a PA himself by completing a year of clinical rotations.

In 1984 he became director of the program, serving until 1999.

Intensely interested in the history of the profession, Carter established an Office for PA History at Duke, and obtained grant funding to create a digital library of source documents for the DUMC Library and Archives. In 2002, together with Dr. Jeffrey Heinrich, he established the Society for the Preservation of Physician Assistant History (now the PA History Society), and served as its Executive Director until his retirement in 2007.

A widely published author on PA workforce issues, Carter has served on the Boards of the NCCPA and the PA Foundation. He has twice received the Presidential Award from the AAPA (2001 and 2007). He is currently the Historian Emeritus of the History Society.

1986

With the encouragement and the support of the AAPA, the Omnibus Budget Reconciliation Act, PL 99-210, is signed into law. It provides **reimbursement** under Medicare, Part B, for PA services in hospitals and nursing homes, and for assisting in surgery.

Physician Assistants: New Models of Utilization, edited by Sarah E. Zarbock and **Kenneth Harbert, PhD, PA-C**, is published by Praeger Publishers.

APAP begins work on the "PA of the Year 2000" project in cooperation with the AAPA. Led by Jack Liskin, APAP President, six work groups convene in New Orleans in October to develop recommendations relevant to PA practice and education for the year 2000.

1987

National PA Day, October 6th, is established, coinciding with the 20th anniversary of the first graduating class of PAs from the Duke University PA Program, and, coincidentally, the birthday of **Eugene A. Stead, Jr., MD**.

The new AAPA National Headquarters at 950 North Washington Street is built and occupied in Alexandria, VA.

Additional Medicare coverage of PA services in rural and other underserved areas is approved by Congress.

1988

The first issue of the *Journal of the American Academy of Physician Assistants* (JAAPA) is published.

AAPA and APAP enter into a fixed-fee contractual arrangement for staffing services, including a part-time

Coordinator of APAP services employed by the AAPA.

The JRC-PA is renamed the **Accreditation Review Committee on Education for the Physician Assistant (ARC-PA)**.

Announcement for the AAPA/APAP
Job Bank in 1985

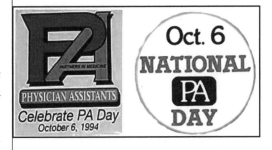

Examples of annual pin designs for
National PA Day

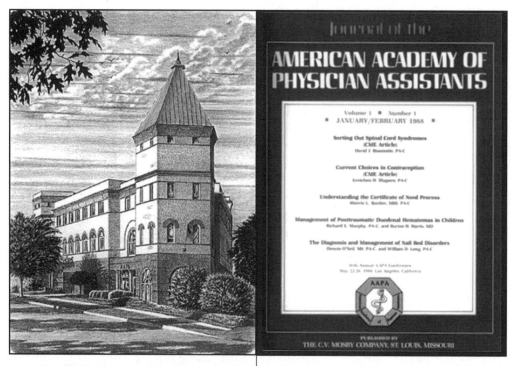

New AAPA Headquarters Building opens in Alexandria, VA, in 1987

Cover of the inaugural issue of JAAPA

1989

The newsletter, *Perspective on PA Education*, is published by APAP. Mike Huckabee, PA-C, is chosen to serve as Editor.

Physician Assistants for the Future, an in-depth study of PA education and practice in the year 2000, begun in 1986, is published by APAP.

AAPA and APAP collaborate to publish *A Guide for Institutions Interested in Creating New Physician Assistant Educational Programs*.

US Navy and Public Health Service PAs are granted commissioned officer rank.

1990

NCCPA and AAPA assign a joint task force to develop "Pathway II," a take-home version of the recertification examination.

The APAP revises and publishes the *National Directory of Physician Assistant Programs: 1990-92* to help individuals interested in becoming physician assistants locate and apply to PA educational programs.

END OF THE DECADE

Number of programs **accredited**: 45

Number of physician assistants initially **certified**: 21,194

Emblems used by the US Navy and the
US Public Health Service

ADDITIONAL PA LEADERS OF THE DECADE

BURDEEN CAMP, PA-C

Burdeen Camp graduated in 1973 from the first Yale PA Program class and has been an ambassador for the Program and the Profession ever since. She was the founding secretary of Yale's Jack W. Cole PA Student Society and past president of the Connecticut APA. She has held multiple leadership roles in the House of Delegates of AAPA including speaker and Vice President. She helped create the infrastructure that allowed AAPA to grow and flourish. Burdeen helped ensure that the formerly male dominated PA profession embraced women equally. An outstanding clinician and teacher, she spent most of her career in Medical Oncology at Yale New Haven Hospital, including management responsibilities at the McGivney Center for Cancer Care. She is the recipient of the inaugural Distinguished Alumna Award of the Yale PA Program.

R. SCOTT CHAVEZ, PhD, MPA, PA

A former Speaker of the AAPA House of Delegates, Scott Chavez served as President in 1986-87. During his term, partly through his efforts, PAs secured Medicare coverage of services provided in hospitals and nursing homes; National PA Day, October 6th, was established; and AAPA moved into the new headquarters it had built in Alexandria, VA. He was active with the Minority Affairs Committee, establishing Project Access, a program providing outreach to high school and junior college students interested in pursuing a career as a PA. During the years following his presidency, he became the longtime vice president of the National Commission on Correctional Health Care, and a national authority on prison health needs. Dr. Chavez passed away on March 7, 2013.

ANN DAVIS, MS, PA-C

Ann Davis graduated from of the University of Colorado physician assistant program in 1978, practiced in Arizona and California, and then taught at the University of Colorado PA Program. For many years Ann served as a volunteer leader in AAPA, and in state organizations in Arizona and California, focusing her efforts on development of state laws for PAs. She has served as President of the Arizona State Association of PAs. In 1994 Ann joined the AAPA staff as director of state government affairs. Her role is to advocate for improvements in state regulation of PAs, and to educate state and national groups on best practices in utilization and regulation. She is currently Senior Director, Constituent Organization Outreach and Advocacy.

DANA R. GRAY, PA-C

Dana Gray is a graduate of Case Western Reserve University who learned about the PA concept during service as an Army Medical Corpsman. He has practiced in cardiovascular surgery for more than 30 years. One of the early pioneers the harvesting of veins, he performed the first vein procedure using an endoscope. Dana worked in trauma, as well, managing patients throughout their hospitalization. Notably, he cared for patients in the office in association with his supervising physician, Dr. Jonathan Hill. Gray and Hill received the AAPA Physician - PA Partnership Award in 2012. Dana's many PA leadership positions include President of the Association of PAs in Cardiovascular Surgery, President of the Oregon Academy of Physician Assistants, member of the Oregon State Medical Board, and Chair of the Oregon Board's PA Committee for 20 years.

KENNETH R. HARBERT, PHD, MHA, PA-C

Ken Harbert is a graduate of the SUNY-Stony Brook PA program and is one of the first PAs to work in psychiatry. Over the past 25 years, he has helped establish eight PA programs in the USA and assisted the Netherlands to develop their PA profession. While a clinical administrator at the Geisinger Medical Center in Danville, PA, Harbert wrote some of the first guidelines for use of PAs in hospitals. As a former corpsman, he founded, and served as executive director of the Veterans Caucus for 20 years, writing extensively about their history. He has served on numerous national committees within AAPA, NCCPA, the PA Foundation, the Health Services Administration, and the Department of Defense. He is a charter board member of the Pennsylvania Society of PAs, the Maryland Academy of PAs, the DC Chapter of PAs, and the Association of Post Graduate PA Programs.

P. EUGENE JONES, PHD, PA-C

Eugene Jones, a 1975 graduate of the US Navy/ University of Nebraska PA Program, remained in the US Navy as a PA until 1989. Since 1993, he has chaired the Department of PA Studies at the University of Texas Southwestern Medical Center in Dallas. Dr. Jones is a past president of PAEA and former Editor-in-Chief of the *Journal of Physician Assistant Education* (JPAE). He has served on the editorial board of JAAPA and chaired many PAEA committees including the PAEA Research Institute. Dr. Jones received the PAEA Research Achievement award in 2007. His articles in *JAMA* and *Academic Medicine* have kept medical colleagues informed of the PA profession's growth and development. He is a Distinguished Teaching Professor, and an elected member of the Southwestern Academy of Teachers and the UT Academy of Health Science Education.

RON NELSON, PA-C

Ron L. Nelson, an informally trained PA, co-founded and served as the first president of the National Association of Rural Health Clinics. He served twice as President of AAPA, and was appointed by President George W. Bush to serve on the National Advisory Committee on Rural Health & Human Services. He is also a past president of the PA History Society. At the time of his death in 2011, Nelson was President of Health Services Associates and a recognized expert in the area of reimbursement and physician payment related to rural health clinics and federally qualified health centers. He also worked as a PA for Spectrum Health Gerber Memorial and was on faculty for Central Michigan University's PA program. He received the Gettel Award in 2010 given for "outstanding leadership and commitment to the health of Michigan's rural residents."

CARL TONEY, PA

Carl Toney, a former corpsman, graduated from the Duke University program in 1979. He has held faculty positions at Duke, Emory, and the University of New England. In addition to practicing clinically in primary care, Toney has made significant contributions in the areas of public policy serving as a consultant to the National Health Service Corps, as a health manpower specialist for the Georgia State Office of Rural Health, as a U.S. Public Health Service Primary Care Policy Fellow, and as Director of the Office on AIDS & Sexually Transmitted Disease Prevention, Maine Bureau of Health. He is Past President, Association of Clinicians for the Underserved. For his outstanding efforts to bring primary care to medically underserved communities, Toney was featured in *Big Doctoring in America – Profiles in Primary Care* by Fitzhugh Mullan, M.D.

1991-2000

Maturation and Growth

During the decade of the 1990s, there is sharp growth in the number of accredited programs from 45 to 114. Most of the new programs appear in smaller colleges affiliated with community hospitals. As applications soar, the vast majority of students admitted already possess a baccalaureate degree. The result is a trend toward the award of the Master's degree to graduating PAs. In a reversal from past experience, the majority of applicants are now women. Employment opportunities far exceed the number of graduates. VA medical centers, the Military, and other state and Federally-sponsored health institutions rely heavily on PAs to bolster medical staffs. Published studies lead to greater HMO reliance on PAs to reduce cost. States continue to revise legislation, rules and regulations in order to enhance the effectiveness of PAs. The Balanced Budget Act of 1997 recognizes PAs as covered providers in all settings at a uniform rate of payment. The last of the branches of the military service grant commissioned status to PAs. Mississippi becomes the last of the states to authorize physicians to delegate the practice of medicine to PAs. Administrative responsibility for ARC-PA is transferred from the AMA to AAPA; the corporate office moves to Marshfield, WI. The NCCPA examination is administered by computer in a move toward administration throughout the calendar year.

1991

With the concurrence of the AMA, the AAPA assumes administrative responsibility of the **Accreditation Review Committee on Education for Physician Assistants** (ARC-PA, formerly the JRC-PA). **John McCarty**, Treasurer of Committee, and a physician assistant at the Marshfield Clinic, assumes the role of Executive Director, initially on a part-time basis. He becomes the first PA to become CEO of any of the major PA governing bodies. The corporate offices of the ARC-PA move to Marshfield, Wisconsin.

The Student Academy Challenge Bowl is founded to offer a *"Jeopardy-style"* competition for PA students at the AAPA Annual Conference.

Clinician Reviews is published as the first clinical journal targeting PAs and NPs. David Mittman, PA-C, co-founder

JOHN E. McCARTY, MPAS, PA

John McCarty is Executive Director of the Accreditation Review Commission on Education for the Physician Assistant (ARC-PA), a position he has held for 22 years. He is the first, and, thus far the only, PA to serve as the Chief Executive Officer of any of the profession's governing organizations.

A graduate of the program at Cuyahoga Community College, McCarty was employed by the Marshfield Clinic in Marshfield, WI, where he worked in general surgery, specializing in pediatric oncology. He soon became involved in medical education, sequentially assuming administrative responsibility for programs in graduate and student education, continuing medical education, and corporate education. He ultimately served as the Administrative Director of the Marshfield Clinic Division of Education.

Having been appointed to the ARC-PA in 1985, he had been serving as Treasurer for four years when, in 1991, the American Medical Association was seeking an organization to contract for PA accreditation management. Marshfield accepted the responsibility, naming McCarty as the part-time Executive Director. As the number of programs grew and the processes became more complex, the organization became independent, John assumed full time responsibility, and, in 2004, the ARC-PA corporate office relocated to Johns Creek, GA, adjacent to the offices of the NCCPA.

During McCarty's tenure at ARC-PA, the number of accredited programs has grown from 54 to more than 170 with as many as 75 more being overseen through their planning stages.

of Clinicians Publishing Group, becomes Editor-in-Chief.

1992

US Army and **US Coast Guard** PAs are commissioned.

The AAPA and the APAP Boards of Directors begin the first of a series of annual joint planning meetings.

The APAP **faculty development scholarship** is established.

The APAP offers the first of a series of workshops for institutions considering the development of new Physician Assistant programs.

1993

The Role of the Physician Assistant and Nurse Practitioner in Primary Care, edited by Kay Clawson and Marian Osterwise, is published by the Association of Academic Health Centers.

The first pilot test administration of **NCCPA's Pathway II** recertification examination is offered as an alternative to the proctored PANRE.

Advance for Physician Assistants is published to provide PAs with the latest in practice and clinical information.

The US Army begins commissioning PAs in 1992. Capt. Tom Stanton gives medicine to a Guatamalan girl.

The AAPA is granted observer status in the **House of Delegates of the American Medical Association**.

1994

Physician Assistants: A Guide to Clinical Practice, the first formal textbook intended for PA education, edited by Ruth Ballweg, Sherry Stolberg, and Edward Sullivan, is published by W.B. Saunders Company, Philadelphia, PA.

The AMA's **Committee on Allied Health and Accreditation (CAHEA)** is replaced by the **Commission on Accreditation of Allied Health Education Programs (CAAHEP)**, and becomes the overarching accrediting body that includes the accreditation of PA programs.

RUTH BALLWEG, MPA, PA-C

Ruth Ballweg is Professor and Director of the MEDEX Northwest Physician Assistant Division in the Department of Family Medicine at the University Of Washington School Of Medicine. She has been an acknowledged leader within the PA profession for more than two decades. She has served as President of the Washington Academy of Physician Assistants, and of PAEA. She has been a Commissioner of the NCCPA, and was an inaugural member of the Board of the NCCPA Foundation. She has twice been elected President of the Physician Assistant History Society, and currently serves as its Historian.

A graduate of the MEDEX program, Ms. Ballweg joined the MEDEX faculty in 1981, and became its Director four years later. She oversaw its growth from a 20-student certificate program to a 110-student baccalaureate/master's degree program with multiple training sites serving five rural states in the Pacific Northwest. As an authority on primary care workforce issues she has consulted with the PEW Health Professions Commission, the National Health Service Corps, and HRSA's Title VII Advisory Committee. Widely published, she is the lead editor of *Physician Assistant: A Guide to Clinical Practice*, the first textbook written for PA students, now in its 5th edition.

Ballweg has been notably active in the international development of the PA concept, working with governments and universities in South Africa, Australia, Canada, and Ghana, among others.

Ms. Ballweg was honored by the AAPA for lifetime work in 2012 with the Eugene A. Stead, Jr., Award of Achievement.

Ballweg, Stolberg, and Sullivan book cover; W.B. Saunders, Philadelphia; 1994.

1995

"Physician Assistants in the Health Workforce 1994," a report by the Advisory Group on PAs and the Workforce (AGPAW) is published by the Health Resources and Services Administration, Bureau of Health Professions.

APAP establishes **PATH (Program Assistance and Technical Help)** to provide guidance to new and developing programs.

RODERICK S. HOOKER, PhD, MBA, PA

Rod Hooker has been a leader in research for more than three decades. His interests are medical economics and health policy. He has authored more than 200 publications, as well as books, book chapters, and reports. He is the lead author of *Physician Assistants in American Medicine*, co-authored with James F. Cawley, now in its 3rd Edition. It is a valuable resource for those interested in the origins, education, and employment of physician assistants.

A former hospital corpsman in the US Navy, Hooker served in the Peace Corps in the Kingdom of Tonga before attending the PA Program at St. Louis University. He received an MBA from City University in Seattle, and a PhD in health policy from the Hatfield School Government at Portland State University in Portland OR. For two decades he served as a PA in rheumatology with Kaiser Permanente while studying with Jane Cassels Record, author of the first systemic studies of PAs. Dr. Hooker is known for his active promotion of PA health workforce research. He has worked to be certain that PAs are included in international health entities. He has mentored many PAs into research roles. He developed the infrastructure for rheumatology research within the VA, including longitudinal registries and databases.

Hooker has received the Recognition of Excellence Award from the Kaiser Permanente Northwest Region, and a Research Achievement Award from the Physician Assistant Education Association.

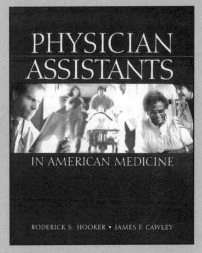

Hooker and Cawley book cover; Churchill Livingston, New York; 1997.

The *Surgical Physician Assistant Journal* is published as a joint effort of the Association of PAs in Cardiovascular Surgery, the American Association of Surgeon Assistants, and PAs in Orthopedic Surgery.

1996

APAP develops and publishes **PACKRAT** (PA Clinical Knowledge Rating and Assessment Tool), a student self-assessment examination, to specifically identify areas of strengths and weaknesses.

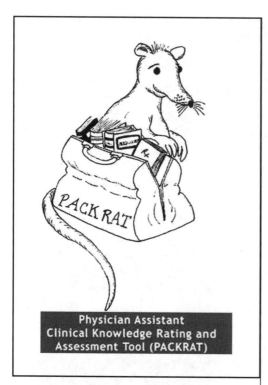

PACKRAT Title and Logo

1997

Physician Assistants in American Medicine, by **Roderick Hooker** and **James Cawley**, is published. It is the second textbook, intended for PAs, to be written or edited by physician assistants.

The **NCCPA redesigns PANCE**, eliminating clinical skills problems (CSPs) because of the complexity and cost of administration at the designated test centers. At the same time it eliminates the extended core components in primary care and surgery. Instead, it introduces a new "stand-

alone" **Surgery Examination**, allowing PAs to earn "special recognition." For the first time the examination is offered twice each year – once in the spring, and once in the fall.

APAP develops a **Research Institute and Endowment Fund** to support PA faculty research initiatives.

The Balanced Budget Act of 1997 recognizes PAs, for the first time, as covered providers in all settings at a uniform rate of payment.

1998

Perspective on PA Education becomes the official peer-reviewed Journal of the Association of Physician Assistant Programs. **Donald Pedersen, Ph.D., PA-C**, is named Editor-in-Chief.

Pathway II pilot testing is completed, and the alternative examination is administered by the NCCPA as a formal alternative to PANRE.

The NCCPA begins requiring PAs **to pass the recertifying examination** within two attempts.

The APAP **Faculty Development Institute** is established to provide oversight to all APAP sponsored faculty development activities.

Confusion's Masterpiece: The Development of the Physician Assistant

DONALD M. PEDERSEN, PhD, PA-C

Don Pedersen, Professor of Family and Preventive Medicine at the University of Utah, recently retired as the longtime Director of the University's Physician Assistant Program. He is a Past President of PAEA. During his tenure on the Board he founded its official journal, *Perspectives on Physician Assistant Education* (now, the *Journal of Physician Assistant Education*), and served as Editor for its first seven years. In addition, he created PAEA's Research Institute, which provides small grants for educational research for PA program faculty; and established a liaison position with the Society of Teachers of Family Medicine.

Pedersen has served as President of the Physician Assistant Foundation, the philanthropic arm of AAPA; following eight years of service as a Trustee he was awarded "Emeritus" status. He was a founding member of the Board of the Physician Assistant History Society. For 10 years he was a member of the Utah Physician Assistant Licensing Board, serving two of those years as Chair. He is currently on the Board of the NCCPA Health Foundation.

Pedersen has been active in international outreach, pioneering the Utah PA Program's clinical activity in Papua New Guinea, and Thailand. Following the 2004 tsunami, he traveled to Southern Thailand where 4000 bodies were processed, helping to identify the dead through DNA samples.

Don's career of stellar service has yielded numerous awards, including Educator of the Year from AAPA, the President's Award from PAEA, and the Distinguished Service Award from the Utah Medical Association.

Profession by Natalie Holt is published (Bull.Hist.Med. 1998, 72:246-278). Extensive interviews with Eugene Stead, Harvey Estes, and others, and her review of Thelma Ingles' papers, reveal details of the clinically successful **nurse clinician** program at Duke University in the 1950s that failed accreditation by the National League for Nursing (NLN). The result led to the initiation of physician assistant training in the next decade.

1999

The NCCPA's Physician Assistant National Certifying Examination (PANCE) is administered for the first time by computer at multiple sites around the country through a process developed by the National Board of Medical Examiners, and already in place for the licensing of physicians. The **"Computer Based Examination"** soon becomes universal for certification

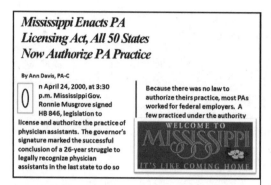

Mississippi Enacts PA Licensing Act, All 50 States Now Authorize PA Practice

By Ann Davis, PA-C

On April 24, 2000, at 3:30 p.m. Mississippi Gov. Ronnie Musgrove signed HB 846, legislation to license and authorize the practice of physician assistants. The governor's signature marked the successful conclusion of a 26-year struggle to legally recognize physician assistants in the last state to do so

Because there was no law to authorize theirs practice, most PAs worked for federal employers. A few practiced under the authority

WELCOME TO

IT'S LIKE COMING HOME

Mississippi becomes the final state to enact PA legislation, May 1999.

and licensure of all health professionals throughout the country.

APAP develops and releases **GRADRAT** (Graduate Rating and Assessment Tool), a self-assessment examination, designed to help certified PAs prepare for the PANRE.

Mississippi enacts legislation authorizing PAs to practice in the state, after 25 years of effort by local and national organizations. Physician assistant practice is finally universally accepted in all of the states and territories of the nation.

The NCCPA's Physician Assistant National Recertifying Examination (PANRE) and Surgery Examination are administered for the first time by computer.

NCCPA launches a new web-based **CME logging system** and provides secure access for all PA-C designees to their certification maintenance record.

AAPA receives clarification from the **Joint Commission on Accreditation of Healthcare Organizations (JCAHO)** that physicians may delegate the performance of history and physical examinations to physician assistants.

END OF THE DECADE

Number of programs **accredited: 114**

Number of physician assistants initially **certified: 45,847**

ADDITIONAL PA LEADERS OF THE DECADE

REAMER BUSHARDT, PHARMD, PA-C

Reamer Bushardt, a tenured professor and Chairman of the Department of PA Studies at Wake Forest University (WFU), works with patients who are experiencing medication-related problems, or have failed to achieve full therapeutic benefits. Many of his publications are on drug safety. He is editor-in-chief for the *JAAPA* and author of the *2005 Medication Update for the Health Professional*. After earning his doctorate of pharmacy from the University of South Carolina, he obtained a PA degree from the Medical University of South Carolina (MUSC). He was director of the PA division at MUSC prior to joining the WFU faculty in 2010. He was recognized in 2013 as one of the "40 leaders under 40" by the Greater Triad Business Journal.

BARRY CASSIDY, PHD, PA-C

A former Air Force corpsman, Barry Cassidy graduated from the Duke University PA Program in 1971. Following two years with the George Washington University program, he practiced as a PA for 20 years before continuing his education. He received a PhD in Bioethics from Union University in Ohio in 1995, and then founded the Midwestern University PA Program in Glendale AZ. He left the program in 2000 when he was appointed Executive Director of the Arizona State Medical Board, the first PA ever to hold such a position. During his tenure, he served on several committees of the Federation of State Medical Boards. At the age of 60, he decided to change careers altogether, becoming an officer with the Phoenix Police Department as a detective in the Family Investigations Bureau.

JAMES F. CAWLEY, MPH, PA-C

A graduate of the Touro College PA Program, James Cawley received an MPH degree at Johns Hopkins University. He is an educator and prolific writer, having co-authored four books and numerous articles about the PA profession. He is Professor and Chair of the Department of Prevention and Community Health in the School of Public Health at the George Washington University. He has served as President of PAEA, and of the PA Foundation, and has been a commissioner of the NCCPA. A member of numerous advisory committees, he has been Chair of the Editorial Board of the Journal of the AAPA, and of the AAPA's Research Advisory Committee. He has twice been named Outstanding PA of the Year by the AAPA, and in 2011 received its prestigious Eugene A. Stead Award of Achievement.

RANDY D. DANIELSON, PHD, PA-C

Randy Danielson, a former Air Force corpsman, who then joined the Army National Guard, completed his total military service in 1998 as a Lt. Colonel, and veteran of Desert Storm. A Utah MEDEX Program graduate, he earned an MS at Nebraska, and a PhD at Union University. He taught at Wichita State, and at A.T. Still University, in Mesa, AZ, where he is Dean of the School of Health Sciences. He has served AAPA as vice-speaker of the HOD, President of the Veteran's Caucus, and member of the Board of Directors. A commissioner of the NCCPA for several years, he became Chair of the Board, and later led the NCCPA Foundation as its Senior Vice President. He is a prolific writer of articles, book chapters and one book, and the long-time Editor of Clinician Reviews. He has twice been appointed to the Arizona Regulatory Board for PAs, serving as its chair in 2002-04.

BRUCE C. FICHANDLER, PA

Bruce Fichandler retired in 2012 from the Board of Directors of AAPA after 32 years, the longest that anyone has served that organization. His roles included President, Treasurer and VP/Speaker of the House of Delegates. He was a highly decorated US Army combat medic in Vietnam and a graduate of the second Yale PA Program class. He worked clinically in the Yale Plastic Surgery Section, with a particular interest in the care of burn patients and became co-director of the Norwalk Hospital/Yale University PA Surgical Residency in 1988. He has been a leader of the Connecticut Academy of PAs and is well known for his prodigious volunteer service for MADD, the Special Olympics, and the Connecticut Food Bank. He is the recipient of many awards from national, regional and local organizations and institutions.

PAUL LOMBARDO MPS, PA-C

Paul Lombardo graduated from Stony Brook's first PA class in 1973 and retired as Clinical Associate Professor and Chair of the Department of Physician Assistant Education there in 2012. He received his master's degree at New School in NYC. Paul was a dynamic leader at Stony Brook, a very successful fundraiser, and is a multi-published author. He holds the remarkable distinction as the only PA to have served on the governing boards of all four PA national organizations: AAPA, PAEA, ARC-PA and NCCPA. He is the recipient of the New York State Student PA Society's Outstanding Teacher Award, AAPA's Distinguished Service Award, and PAEA's Outstanding Professional Service Award, among others. His many interests include governance, fostering leadership, mental health training initiatives and international learning. opportunities.

WILLIAM H. MARQUARDT, MA, PA-C

Bill Marquardt has been a leader of the Profession throughout his forty year career. He was as an Air Force Pharmacy technician prior to being accepted for PA training at Sheppard AFB in Texas. He received a Bachelor's Degree in from the University of Nebraska in 1976 and a Masters Degree in Health Care Administration from Central Michigan University. He served as AAPA President, after having been a Director-at-Large, and Secretary for two terms. He was Secretary Treasurer of PAEA and on the Board of Directors of the Student Academy of AAPA. He has been active with the PA History Society and completed a three year term as President in 2011. He is currently Associate Professor and Associate Dean for Physician Assistant Education at Nova Southeastern University in Ft. Lauderdale, FL. where he is responsible for PA training at its four campuses.

DAVID E. MITTMAN, PA-C

David Mittman, a leader and advocate for PAs, and later NPs, was a medic in the Air Force Reserves when he graduated from the Long Island University (LIU) Brooklyn Hospital Center PA Program in 1975. He is a founding member of the NY State Society of PAs, serving as its president in 1979. From 1981 to 1983, he served on the AAPA Board of Directors. Professionally, he helped improve PA legislation in New York and later in New Jersey, calling for a march of PAs on Trenton, the State Capital in 1988. In 1990, he cofounded the Clinicians Group to publish *Clinician Reviews* and *Clinician News* and with his partners built the organization into a major publishing business by launching eight journals in six different physician specialties within an eight year period, something never done before in the history of medical publishing.

JOHN PADGETT, MS, PhD, PA

John Padgett, a Special Forces medic during the Vietnam War, graduated from the University of Washington MEDEX program in 1973. His 25 years of clinical experience include family practice, urgent care and industrial medicine. He has spent many years in humanitarian work with assignments in the U.S. Trust Territories of the Pacific, and in Nicaragua, and Iraq. He has served 35 years in US Army Special Operations, active and reserve, receiving numerous awards for valor and service. John holds an MS from St. Francis University, and a Doctorate in Health Science from St. George University. He has served as a clinical coordinator and educator with several PA programs. He has been President of the AAPA Veterans' Caucus, and a delegate to the AAPA HOD. He was an invited participant at the White House discussion on PTSD in January, 2012.

JUSTINE STRAND DE OLIVEIRA, DrPH, PA-C

Justine Strand de Oliveira graduated from the Duke University PA Program in 1981 and received her doctorate in public health from the UNC at Chapel Hill in 2008. Her clinical practice is in public health and family medicine. She is a member of the Duke University Medical School faculty, former chief of the PA Education Division, and currently professor and Vice Chair for Education in the Department of Community and Family Medicine. She is a former member of the North Carolina Institute of Medicine, serves on the Advisory Council for the North Carolina Center for Nursing, and is a past president of the North Carolina Medical Society Foundation. She has been a US Public Health Service Primary Care Policy Fellow, and a Past President of PAEA. She was awarded Outstanding PA of the Year by the AAPA in 2005.

GREG P. THOMAS, MPH, PA

Greg Thomas received his baccalaureate degree as a PA from the Baylor College of Medicine, and an MPH from the University of Texas, School of Public Health. Following two years as a PA educator in Texas, he moved to the George Washington University in the field of continuing medical education, where he remained for 13 years. He became Director of the Office of CME, and a national leader, as a member of the Board of the Alliance for Continuing Medical Education, the only PA ever to hold such positions in medical education. In 1992 he joined the staff of AAPA, serving in a number of roles, ultimately becoming Senior Vice President for Education, Membership and Development. Leaving AAPA in 2011, he has become a consultant to both NCCPA and PAEA, serving both in the areas of professional development and strategic alliances.

PEGGY VALENTINE, RN, EdD, PA

As a Howard University PA graduate with prior experience as an RN, Peggy Valentine has achieved a distinguished career. As a member of the Howard faculty, she served as chair of the PA Education Department and Director of the National AIDS Minority Information and Education Program. She is the recipient of the 1997 AAPA Paragon "Educator of the Year" award. Currently, she is Dean of the School of Health Sciences at Winston-Salem State University. Her many international projects include chair of the Consortium on International Management Policy and Development, and university liaison with Hubei University of Chinese Medicine. She has directed projects in Malawi and Zimbabwe. She has held leadership roles with the Association of Schools of Allied Health where she is a distinguished fellow.

2001-2010

GOING INTERNATIONAL

As the new programs developed in the last decade grow and expand, record numbers of PAs take the certifying examination. As the profession celebrates its 40th anniversary, international interest in the PA model of health care delivery grows with the establishment of PA educational programs in seven countries. In 2001, ARC-PA becomes a freestanding accreditation agency. APAP launches a Central Application Service for Physician Assistants. The Physician Assistant History Society is established in Durham, NC in 2002. Increasing numbers of PAs are appointed to positions in Federal agencies, and in 2004, two PAs are elected to state legislatures. In 2005, APAP changes its name to the Physician Assistant Education Association; a year later the organization holds its first meeting outside the United States in Quebec, CAN. ARC-PA awards accreditation to two postgraduate programs, and the US Army and Baylor University create the first doctoral degree program. New regulations limiting the number of hours that medical residents may work without relief opens the door to expanding opportunities for PAs in hospital settings. In 2010 President Obama signs the Patient Protection and Affordable Care Act, potentially adding 20-30 million patients to the ranks of the insured population.

2001

ARC-PA, now called the **Accreditation Review Commission on Education for the Physician Assistant**, begins operation as a freestanding accreditation agency for the physician assistant profession.

NCCPA offers a second administration of PANRE and Pathway II each year, and implements new certification maintenance requirements to end the practice of renewing certificates for PAs who fail the examination.

NCCPA announces that it will now assume responsibility for recording all CME hours for purposes of re-registration of certificates, and recertification, ending 25 years of service by AAPA as an intermediary. AAPA will continue to approve educational activities for credit.

APAP launches a **Central Application Service for Physician Assistants (CASPA)**. CASPA provides PA applicants a convenient, state-of-the-art, web-based application service that allows them to apply to any number of participating PA programs by completing a single application.

The **Physician Assistant History Office** is established in Durham, NC, as a joint effort of the Department of Community and Family Medicine, Duke University Medical Center and the AAPA, APAP

Since April 2001, PAEA has offered the Central Application Service for Physician Assistants (CASPA), which provides a simplified online process of applying to physician assistant (PA) programs. Applicants complete one application and submit it with corresponding materials to the centralized service, which is provided by Liaison International. CASPA verifies the application components for accuracy, calculates the applicant's grade point averages (GPA), and sends the materials to the PA programs that the applicant designates.

PAEA establishes a Central Application Service, permitting applicants to apply to multiple programs with a single application.

and NCCPA. The office is dedicated to study, preserve and present the history of the PA profession.

The first PA programs are started in The Netherlands at University of Utrecht and the Academy of Healthcare Arnhem/Nijmegen.

2002

Representatives from the AAPA, ARC-PA, APAP, and NCCPA begin regular meetings to share mutual interests related to the PA profession.

The **Physician Assistant History Society** is incorporated (as the Society for the Preservation of Physician Assistant History, Inc.) for education, research, and literary purposes. The Society's mission is to foster the preservation, study and presentation of the history

APAP/PAEA celebrates its 30th Anniversary. Shown here (from left) are Thomas Piemme, the second President; Suzanne Greenberg; the first Secretary; and Donald Fisher, the first Executive Director at their panel presentation in Miami, FL.

Cover of the 35th anniversary issue of the Journal of the American Academy of Physician Assistants, now indexed by the National Library of Medicine.

of the physician assistant profession. The Society's Board of Directors meets for first time in Boston, MA. **Jeffrey Heinrich, EdD, PA,** is elected President; **Reginald Carter, PhD, PA,** is appointed as the Executive Director, and official Historian.

A special issue of **JAAPA** chronicles the 35th anniversary of the graduation of the first formally-trained PAs in 1967.

Canadian, Dutch and British delegations meet during the AAPA's Annual Conference in Boston.

APAP celebrates its 30th Anniversary at the Education Forum held in Miami. **Pioneering Leaders** including **Thomas Piemme, MD, Donald Fisher, PhD,**

and **Suzanne Greenberg, MS**, reminisce about the founding of the Association and the establishment of the AAPA/APAP national office.

The **Accreditation Council on Graduate Medical Education (ACGME)** affirms its policy to limit medical and surgical resident working hours in order to reduce fatigue and stress. A byproduct is an increase in opportunities for PAs in the hospital setting.

J. JEFFREY HEINRICH, EdD, PA

Jeff Heinrich was a co-founder, together with Reginald Carter, of the Physician Assistant History Society, and served as its first President. His history of leadership began when, as a student, he was selected to serve on the Board of the AAPA, and became the first President of what was to become the Student Academy.

A native of Vermont, Heinrich entered military service in 1964, and served as a hospital corpsman with the United States Marines in Vietnam, earning a Combat Operation Medal, and a Purple Heart, among other military honors. Following service, he finished college, and taught middle school before entering the Duke University PA Program in 1971. Upon graduation, he began his career at Yale University in the Department of Plastic Surgery where he was a burn specialist. After obtaining a doctoral degree in education, he moved on to the George Washington University, where he became the Program Director, and rose to the rank of full Professor.

Heinrich has served as President of both the Connecticut Academy of Physician Assistants, and the District of Columbia Academy of Physician Assistants. He has been elected to the Board of Directors of the AAPA, and has served as its Treasurer. He has been a President of the Physician Assistant Foundation, and an Associate Editor of the *PA Journal*.

To honor his service, he received the Distinguished Service Award from the AAPA in 1985.

2003

The Centers for Medicare and Medicaid Services (CMS) expands the ability of PAs to have an ownership interest in a practice under the Medicare program.

A PA program at Base Borden in Ontario becomes the **first accredited PA program in Canada**. PAs are introduced in England through a government sponsored pilot project.

For the first time, three PAs among 34 candidates are selected as **Primary Health Care Fellows** by the Department of Health and Human Services.

More than 99 percent of the PAs whose 2000-2002 Category I CME hours are audited, pass the NCCPA's inaugural CME audit.

The **Canadian Medical Association recognizes the PA profession** as a designated health profession, eligible for the CMA accreditation.

Although appointment to Federal agencies had occurred previously (most notably to the National Health Service

Corps), PAs are now regularly appointed to **Federal Advisory Committees** by the Department of Health and Human Services. The committees oversee areas of medicine of particular interest to the PA profession, e.g., primary care training, rural health initiatives, and human services. PAs are included as members of the Title 7 Advisory Committee.

2004

Karen Bass, PA-C, of California and **Mark Hollo, PA-C**, of North Carolina, become the **first PAs to be elected to state legislatures**.

ARC-PA is awarded recognition as the formal accrediting body for physician assistant education by the Council for Higher Education. Its corporate offices are moved to Johns Creek, GA, in the same building as the headquarters of the NCCPA.

Mark Hollo and Karen Bass are the first PAs to be elected to their respective state legislatures in North Carolina and California.

The annual **Conference of AAPA**, held in Las Vegas, NV, attracts 10,500 registrants – the largest in its history.

2005

A report entitled, *Competencies for the Physician Assistant Profession*, is developed jointly, and approved by the four major physician assistant organizations (NCCPA, PAEA, AAPA and ARC-PA).

The member programs of the **Association of Physician Assistant Programs (APAP)** vote to change the organization's name to the **Physician Assistant Education Association (PAEA)**.

The University of Hertfordshire, England, inaugurates the **first PA program in the United Kingdom**. The Netherlands graduates its first class of PAs.

The **US Virgin Islands** approves legislation permitting PAs to be licensed to practice medicine.

Eugene A. Stead, Jr., dies at the age of 96 at his home in North Carolina.

2006

USPHS Rear Admiral Mike Milner becomes the **first PA flag officer**.

The Physician Assistant Education Association (PAEA) moves into new office space in Alexandria, VA, as an independent organization after 36 years of sharing a joint national office with AAPA.

Scotland introduces 12 PAs into a pilot program developed by the National Health Service.

PAEA holds its first annual meeting outside the United States in Quebec City, Canada.

2007

The U.S. Army and Baylor University award the **first clinical doctorate degree (DScPA)** tor Army PAs who successfully complete an 18-month residency in emergency medicine at Brooke Army Medical Center at Fort Sam Houston in San Antonio, TX.

The United States celebrates the **40th anniversary** of the graduation of the first formally trained physician assistants, **Kenneth Ferrell**, **Victor Germino** and **Richard Schelle**.

PAEA celebrates its 35th anniversary as an organization.

Globalization of the PA concept accelerates in several countries, including Australia, Canada, England, the Netherlands, Scotland, South Africa, and Taiwan where medical workers are trained to function under the supervision of a doctor.

Health Force Ontario, an initiative by the Ontario Ministry of Health, begins a pilot program introducing PAs in the province.

Indiana passes legislation allowing PAs to prescribe. **All 50 states**, the District of Columbia, and Guam **now allow PAs to prescribe**.

2008

AAPA celebrates its 40th Anniversary.

Manitoba begins the first civilian Canadian PA program.

For the first time, ARC-PA awards its **accreditation to two postgraduate PA programs**: the University of Texas M. D. Anderson Cancer Center PA Postgraduate Program in Oncology (Houston), and the Johns Hopkins Hospital Postgraduate Surgical Residency for PAs (Baltimore).

The Bureau of Labor Statistics identifies the PA profession as one of 30 occupations expected to grow rapidly over the next decade.

2009

E. Harvey Estes, MD, is awarded the first **Eugene A. Stead, Jr., Award of Achievement** by AAPA.

AAPA and PAEA host a **PA Clinical Doctorate Summit** in Atlanta. Fifty independent representatives, from within and outside the PA profession, discuss whether the clinical doctoral degree should be awarded as a post-graduate degree to PAs. The Summit endorses the master's degree as the terminal degree for PA clinical education. A doctorate degree is reserved for postgraduate education in another discipline.

Queensland, Australia conducts a 1 year pilot sponsored by the Ministry of Health that places 5 US PAs in rural, remote and urban sites. South Australia also implements a pilot for 3 US PAs in surgery.

The University of Queensland opens the first Australian PA Program for experienced health care personnel in Brisbane.

The premier issue of *PA Professional*, an official monthly publication, replacing *AAPA News*, is issued by AAPA in June.

2010

AAPA President Stephen Hanson, PAEA President Kevin Lohenry and six other PAs attend a **White House conference** at which President Barack Obama calls on Congress to take action on health care reform.

AAPA hosts two-day **Research Summit** to initiate a research agenda for the PA profession.

President Obama signs the **Patient Protection and Affordable Care Act** which includes a gradual implementation timeline through 2014. Provisions of the act, when fully established, will add 30 million persons to the ranks of those who are fully insured. The need for additional health manpower, especially in primary care, will be greater than anything seen since the implementation of Medicare and Medicaid in 1966.

New Zealand begins its first PA pilot with two US surgical PAs filling hospitalist roles in a surgical teaching setting.

President Barack Obama signs the Patient Protection and Affordable Care Act. The law provides new vistas of opportunity for physician assistants.

NCCPA hosts its first international meeting at its headquarters in Atlanta to discuss certification, test item banking, and other regulatory issues with international PA program representatives.

AAPA and the American College of Physicians release a policy monograph entitled *Internists and Physician Assistants: Team-based Primary Care* that supports the critical roles PAs and physicians play in improving access to quality primary care.

END OF THE DECADE

Number of programs **accredited: 148**

Number of physician assistants initially **certified: 92,049**

ADDITIONAL PA LEADERS OF THE DECADE

DAVID P. ASPREY, PhD, PA-C

David Asprey is Assistant Dean at the University of Iowa, and Professor and Chair of the Department of Physician Assistant Studies. He holds BA degrees from Bethel University and the University of Iowa PA Program, an MS Degree in Instructional Design and Technology and a PhD in Higher Education. His practice as a PA includes 4 years in emergency medicine and 22 years in pediatric cardiology. He has authored numerous abstracts, articles and chapters, and co-edited 4 textbooks. He has served as President of PAEA, and as Vice Chair of the Federal Advisory Committee on Training in Primary Care Medicine and Dentistry. He is a member of the Institute of Medicine's Committee on Governance and Financing of Graduate Medical Education and is the recipient of several awards including the PAEA's Master Faculty Award.

WILLIAM KOHLHEPP, DHSc, PA-C

Dr. William Kohlhepp graduated in 1979 from the UMDNJ/Rutgers PA Program. He is Associate Professor of Physician Assistant Studies and Associate Dean for the School of Health Sciences at Quinnipiac University. He holds a Doctorate in Health Sciences from Nova Southeastern University. His service to the PA profession began in 1978 when he was National Student Secretary. He currently is Secretary-Treasurer of PAEA and a Past President of the American Academy of Physician Assistants (AAPA), Past Speaker of its House of Delegates, and Past Chair of the AAPA Board. He is also a Past Chair of the NCCPA Board of Directors. He has twice served as Connecticut AAPA President. His chapters on "Professionalism" and the "Physician Assistant Relationship to Physicians" appear in *Physician Assistant: A Guide to Clinical Practice*, 5th ed., 2013.

DAVID KUHNS, MPH, PA-C

David Kuhns served in the US Air force as a Medical Services and Aeromedical Technician. He received his PA training at St. Louis University, followed by an MS in international public health from Boston University. He has a long history in global health and disaster/humanitarian relief, including missions with Doctors Without Borders in Somalia and Afghanistan, a leadership role at the University of Birmingham PA program in the United Kingdom, and consultations for PA development in Saudi Arabia, Australia, Scotland, and Ireland. He is active in the Euro-PA Collaborative, UK Association of PAs, and is certified as a PA in Canada. David has worked in wilderness and emergency medicine in rural Maine, where he also served as a member of the faculty at the University of New England PA Program in Portland.

MICHAEL R. MILNER, DHSc, PA-C

Michael R. Milner, a former Air Force corpsman, and 1982 graduate of the University of Oklahoma PA Program, was commissioned in the USPHS in 1989, rising to become the highest ranking PA in the Corps, retiring as a Rear Admiral, responsible for public health programs in the six states of the New England Region. He is currently Dean of the School of PA Studies at Massachusetts College of Pharmacy and Health Sciences in Boston, MA. Career highlights include Chief PA in the Indian Health Service, and work as one of the five Senior Federal Health Officials for Pandemic Influenza and Bioterrorism. His doctorate is from Nova Southeastern University in Fort Lauderdale, FL. He has been a recipient of the USPHS Distinguished Service Medal, the Assistant Secretary for Health Distinguished Service Award, and the AAPA President's Award.

DAWN MORTON-RIAS, EDD, PA-C

Dawn Morton-Rias, Professor and Dean of the College of Health Related Professions at SUNY Downstate, is a Howard University PA Program graduate and a former PAEA president. She provided community-based primary care and GYN services in NYC, and served as the chief medical officer for a health care for the homeless mobile unit for over a decade. She currently serves on the NY State Board for Medicine and the HRSA Advisory Committee on Training in Primary Care Medicine and Dentistry. She has served as a Commissioner on ARC-PA. Morton-Rias is a recipient of a Fulbright Senior Specialists Award sponsored by the US Department of State's Bureau of Educational and Cultural Affairs, and is the first non-physician to be recognized by the Arthur Ashe Institute for Urban Health.

FREDDI SEGAL-GIDAN, PHD, PA-C

Freddi Segal-Gidan, a PA and gerontologist, is the director of the Rancho/USC Alzheimer's Disease Research Center of California. She is director of the PA postgraduate training fellowship in geriatric neurology at USC. She completed the first clinical fellowship training in geriatrics for a PA in the country at the USC Department of Family Medicine in 1985. Dr. Segal-Gidan was awarded her doctoral degree in gerontology-public policy from the USC Leonard Davis School of Gerontology. She is a sought-after lecturer on a variety of geriatric health topics, including dementia, Alzheimer's disease, stroke, and chronic disease. She has served two terms on California's Alzheimer's Disease Advisory Board, and currently serves as AAPA's liaison to the American Geriatrics Society.

HOWARD STRAKER, MPH, PA-C

Howard Straker is dedicated to improving the health of underserved communities. He is Director of Community Medicine of the George Washington University Physician Assistant Program and teaches in the School of Public Health. He was founding Board Chair of the DC Area Health Education Center, board member of the DC Primary Care Association, and a 2004 HHS Primary Care Policy Fellow. He has worked with numerous projects including community health worker training, the Kids to Health Careers program, and a program to build support for safety net providers. Howard is a graduate of the Yale Physician Assistant Program and the University of North Carolina, School of Public Health. He is a GWU education doctoral candidate. He is President of the DC Academy of PAs, and has served on numerous PA committees.

MARY WARNER, MMSC, PA-C

Mary is the Founding Director of the Boston University PA Program, having been Associate Dean and Program Director for the Yale School of Medicine's PA Program for eight years. She received an MMSc degree from Emory University and practiced in emergency medicine, cardiac and orthopedic surgery. She is a member of the Executive Committee of NCCPA Board of Directors and chairs its Research and Test Development Committee. She is a member of the AAPA Research Group and a past member of the Research Institute of PAEA. She was awarded the PAEA Rising Star Award in 2007. She and her collaborators brought the first CME program to Ugandan Clinical Officers. She leads an active research program focusing on longitudinal career patterns of physician assistants.

2011–Present

Into the Future

The Affordable Care Act doubles the projected need for PAs. PAs are seen as essential components of new health care delivery structures such as "accountable care organizations" and "medical homes." Forbes and Money magazines rate the physician assistant Master's degree as the most desirable advanced degree in terms of employment opportunity, income potential, and job satisfaction. NCCPA develops the concept of a "Certificate of Added Qualification" to meet the need of PAs for a credential in a specialty. The Physician Assistant History Society affiliates with the NCCPA, and moves its office and archive to Johns Creek, GA. PAEA celebrates its 40th anniversary at their annual meeting in Seattle in November 2012. Most significantly, the NCCPA issues its 100,000th certificate. The number of accredited programs exceeds 170 with as many as 50 more currently seeking provisional status. The profession is healthy and growing.

2011

The National Commission on Certification of Physician Assistants (NCCPA) develops **Certificate of Added Qualifications (CAQ)** programs that allow PAs to earn formal recognition of their specialty expertise – in cardiovascular and thoracic surgery, emergency medicine, nephrology, orthopedic surgery and psychiatry. The first CAQ examination is held nationally on September 12, 2011.

The Society for the Preservation of Physician Assistant History (**PA History Society**) becomes a support organization to the National Commission on Certification of Physician Assistants (NCCPA). The Society transfers its archive, library and museum collection from the Duke University Medical Center (DUMC) and the Eugene A. Stead, Jr., Center for Physician Assistants, located

Ribbon cutting ceremony at the opening of the new Physician Assistant History Society office in Atlanta. Pictured (from left) are Ruth Ballweg, Historian; Reginald Carter, Historian Emeritus; and Thomas Piemme, President.

in Durham, NC to the **Society's new headquarters at Johns Creek, GA**, adjacent to NCCPA and ARC-PA national offices. The archival function

Past Presidents of PAEA are honored at the celebration of the 40th Anniversary in Seattle in November, 2012.

of the PA History Center is assumed by the Society.

Montefiore Medical Center celebrates the **40th anniversary** of its surgical physician assistant residency program, the first of its kind in the United States. Since 1971, Montefiore has trained more than 375 surgical PAs.

The position of Chief PA for the Veterans Administration is approved, and Denni Woodmansee, PA-C, is chosen to fill this role.

The American Academy of Physician Assistants relocates its headquarters in Alexandria, VA, vacating the building that the organization constructed and owned since 1987.

U.S. Rep. Karen Bass from California is sworn into the 112th Congress becoming the **first PA to hold a seat in the United States House of Representatives**.

2012

The physician assistant master's degree, for the third consecutive year, is rated by both *Forbes* **and** *Money* **magazines** as the most desirable advanced degree in terms of employment opportunity, income potential, and job satisfaction.

The 40th AAPA Annual Conference is held outside of the United States in **Toronto** – in recognition of the growth of the PA profession in Canada.

The **Physician Assistant Education Association** celebrates the **40th anniversary of its founding** at the Annual Meeting in Seattle. Twenty-two of the past presidents of the Association are honored for their contribution.

2013

Care from the Heart is published by BTW Publishing. It is the memoir of **Thelma**

Care from the Heart
By Thelma Marguerite Ingles

Memoirs of the Remarkable Woman and Pioneering Nurse who Helped Inspire the Duke University Physician Assistant Program and Nursing around the World

Book cover of Thelma Ingles' memoirs, *Care from the Heart*; BTW Publishing, 2013

Ingles, the pioneering nurse educator who worked with Eugene A. Stead, Jr. in the 1950s at Duke University to create a program to train nurses in an expanded clinical role. While the program did not survive accreditation by the NLN, it served as the prototype for the physician assistant training program, developed by Stead in the next decade.

STATUS AT PRESENT (MARCH 2013)

Number of programs **accredited: 170**

Number of physician assistants initially **certified: 105,216**

ADDITIONAL PA LEADERS OF THE DECADE

KAREN BASS, PA

Karen Bass is the first physician assistant to be elected to the US House of Representatives. She was elected in 2010 and again in 2012. A native of Los Angeles, she is a 1982 graduate and former faculty member of the USC Keck School of Medicine Primary Care PA Program. Before her election to the California State Assembly in 2005, she worked as a physician assistant at the Los Angeles County-USC Medical Center for ten years. As a member of the California State Assembly (2005-2010), Bass had the distinction of being the first African American woman elected as Speaker of the House (2008-2010). Bass received the 2010 Profiles in Courage Award by the John F. Kennedy Library Foundation for her bipartisan work in proposing a solution to California's budget crises.

JOHN DAVIS, PA-C

John Davis, a 1973 Duke PA Program graduate, was among the first African Americans to serve on the AAPA Board of Directors. He provided 20 years of continuity and mentoring to AAPA and SAAAPA Minority Affairs Committees, was on the PA Foundation's Development Committee and has represented the TN Academy of PAs in the AAPA HOD for more than 30 years. He is especially recognized for his role as national coordinator of Project Access, an outreach program for minority high school programs. He has chaired or been a member of numerous professional committees and most recently, a commissioner for the NCCPA. He received the AAPA Public Education Achievement Award (1994), and the Outstanding Service Award from the Department of Veteran Affairs (1995). He is an instructor at Christian Brothers University PA Program, Memphis, TN.

BOB MCNELLIS, MPH, PA

Bob McNellis has been the Senior Advisor for Primary Care at the Agency for Healthcare Research and Quality (AHRQ) since November 2012. He had earlier been a Visiting Senior Scholar there from 2011 to 2012 serving as a medical officer supporting the U.S. Preventive Services Task Force. McNellis graduated from the George Washington University PA program in 1990, and worked in a variety of clinical and research settings. He joined the faculty at GWU in 1993, serving as director of research and academic coordinator, and for a while as acting Program Director. He then joined the staff of AAPA where he worked for 12 years, ultimately becoming Vice President for Science and Public Health. While there, he completed a fellowship in primary health care policy in 2003. He is a recipient of the Master Teacher Award from PAEA.

JOSANNE PAGEL, MPAS, PA-C

Josanne Pagel, Executive Director of PAs at the Cleveland Clinic with more than 34 years of clinical experience, is a graduate of the Cuyahoga Community College PA Program. She obtained her master's degree in Psychiatry and Addiction Studies from University of Nebraska. Pagel is a former Peace Corps volunteer who has worked in both medical and surgical specialties. She has been president of the Ohio PA association, and served as the Ohio representative to the AAPA HOD, where she chaired the credentialing process. Pagel is presently the Secretary/Treasurer of the AAPA BOD. She has served as a Trustee for the PA Foundation. She presently chairs the PAs in Administration Conference. She has served on the city council, and ran for the Ohio State House of Representatives.

Going Forward

Nearing the half-century mark for this remarkable profession, as this book goes to press, more than 105,000 PAs have been certified by the NCCPA, and more than 170 active PA programs have been accredited by ARC-PA. There is, once more, an acceleration of program growth, as the profession continues to increase in popularity.

Expectations going forward: The cardinal features of the Patient Protection and Affordable Care Act are to be implemented in 2014. Care for the newly enfranchised, as well as the previously underserved, will place the physician assistant on center stage. There will be even more emphasis on health teams, as the "Centers for Medicare and Medicaid Services" explores global payment to "accountable care organizations" and "medical homes." Emphasis will also be placed on the quality of care.

The Issue of Scope of Practice: Dependence or Independence

As noted in the opening chapter, the ability of PAs to practice to "the full scope of their ability and authority" has been based on their "legally dependent" relationship to physicians. This structure has worked exceedingly well. Does the demand for primary care services give us a reason to change this model? Should non-physicians be permitted to practice independently? Would this be accepted by physicians, medical organizations, and patients? If fewer physicians choose to enter primary care specialties, someone must fill the breach. If PAs and NPs were to be able to practice independently, assuming much of the physician's scope of practice, would the quality of patient care be enhanced or diminished? The answer is unknown, but not unknowable. Experimentation will be necessary. The economics of medical education – two years for the PA vs. seven years for the primary care medical specialties – may force the issue.

Health care teams will certainly be necessary to provide the comprehensive care needed for an aging population with chronic illness. Almost certainly, physician/non-physician ratios will change. At a minimum, physicians will delegate more to alternative providers.

The extraordinary success of the PA concept raises other issues. Is it possible to produce well-trained, highly skilled graduates if the profession continues its rapid rate of expansion? There is already competition for clinical training sites, and for capable and willing preceptors. When does further growth become unwise? Can PA faculty be adequately trained to provide the necessary supervision, and to what extent? Physician preceptorships, the hallmark of PA training, must not be lost. Nursing has been going its own way for generations, evolving into a "guild" model of education. The journey down that path would likely lead to a struggle for independence from medicine.

THE ISSUE OF THE CREDENTIAL: THE CERTIFICATE OF COMPETENCE OR THE EDUCATIONAL DEGREE

From the outset, PA students underwent rigorous education and clinical training, analogous to that for medical students and residents. Upon completion, they received a certificate of achievement from their programs, just as residents do upon completion of their training. PAs then took a national examination, receiving a certificate of competence from the NCCPA. Degrees were seen as irrelevant to the quality of medical care. Most programs offered an optional baccalaureate degree, provided that the student had accrued enough academic credits to qualify. The Master's degree dominates today, largely because most students now enter programs with an undergraduate degree in hand. However, neither degree has any influence on scope of practice.

The competence driven culture of the PA world serves as a contrast to many, if not most, other allied health occupations. What began as hospital-based training, evolved by stages, over time, to what has been called, "degree creep." First the baccalaureate, then the Master's, and now, for some occupations, the doctoral degree, has become the norm. Pharmacy, physical therapy, and occupational therapy now mandate the doctorate to be the entry level qualification for the occupation. Advanced nursing is moving in that direction, closing nurse practitioner Master's degree programs in favor of a Doctor of Nursing Practice (DNP). It would appear to be a quest for status, prestige, and independence (not to mention pay grade). It is difficult, however, to find evidence that the end result is improved patient care.

In 2009, PA professional leaders and educators met at an extraordinary summit in Atlanta to consider the merits of advanced degrees, and the doctoral degree in particular. With virtual unanimity, the idea of the clinical doctorate was rejected. Once again, the PA profession went against the grain of traditional thinking. The PA leaders deserve great credit for their wisdom and restraint.

Given the increase in cost of education, practitioners in these occupations seek higher compensation. Will the NP with a doctorate in nursing practice be able to command a higher salary? It will be the role of the large multispecialty clinics that employ PAs and NPs in great numbers, insurance companies, and government agencies to answer the question.

THE ISSUES OF GENDER AND ALTERNATIVE QUALIFICATIONS FOR ADMISSION TO PROGRAMS

Over the decades more women have entered the PA profession (now more than 70 percent). This is not dissimilar to trends in medicine, law, and business. Remaining to be fully studied is the question of whether the desire to raise a family might influence specialty choice, as it does in medicine.

The military veteran presents a paradox. The PA concept began in most programs with former corpsmen, veterans of the Korean and Vietnam wars. Today, the veterans of Iraq and Afghanistan seek the same opportunity. They must compete for admission, however, with applicants who have substantive formal education. Ways must be found to accommodate their transition to civilian life, as was done in the early days. There is no evidence that a corpsman with less formal education would function any less competently as a physician assistant.

THE ISSUE OF INTERNATIONAL OUTREACH

The US physician assistant movement has begun to move internationally in the new millennium. While emerging African nations have had non-physician clinicians since their revolutions of the late 1970s, their roles did not undergo further development until recently with the help of advisors from the United States.

Developed countries, as well, have begun to appreciate the utility of assistants to improve access and efficiency. American PAs began serving as consultants to provide advice that would adapt the PA model to the health systems and culture of a number of countries. The Netherlands was one of the first to adopt the concept, creating five programs in large regional hospitals, training currently employed health workers to become PAs. A series of "pilot" or "demonstration" projects followed in England; Scotland; Ontario, Canada; Queensland, Australia; and New Zealand. Each pilot/demonstration was accompanied by a structured evaluation strategy that informed subsequent programs. New programs have been developed for the military services in Saudi Arabia, South Africa, Ghana, and Germany.

In each of these countries, the introduction of PAs has stimulated innovation in regulation and payment policies. While there is not yet reciprocity between countries, even in a united Europe, to allow cross-border movement by PAs, there is movement to consider regional certification as a future step in the development of international portability of such a career.

LESSONS LEARNED TO INFORM THE FUTURE

* The PA profession has created opportunities for improved health care that educators and leaders never imagined fifty years ago.

* The physician/physician assistant team facilitates access to care that does not exist in a single provider model.

* The physician assistant concept maximizes human capital, often in a non-traditional role.

* The competency-based generalist education permits flexibility for the PA career, providing maximum adaptability in a changing health care environment.

* Patients value the approachability, the openness of communication, and the ability of PAs to serve as brokers on their behalf.

* The US health care system has major regional differences that are often unrecognized, and that provide new opportunities for PAs.

* A key to the success of the profession has always been training in teams that promote interdependence and mutual respect.

* Competency alone must dictate the criteria for accreditation, certification, and practice opportunities, irrespective of educational credentials.

* Understanding the history of this unconventional and highly successful profession will help ensure its successful future.

APPENDIX A

MAJOR PHYSICIAN ASSISTANT ORGANIZATIONS AND LEADERS

AMERICAN ACADEMY OF PHYSICIAN ASSISTANTS

Past Presidents

1968 - 1969	William D. Stanhope, PA-C
1969 - 1970	William D. Stanhope, PA-C
1970 - 1971	John J. McQueary, PA-C
1971 - 1972	John A. Braun, PA-C
1972 - 1973	Thomas R. Godkins, PA-C
1973 - 1974	Paul F. Moson, PA-C
1974 - 1975	C. Emil Fasser, PA-C
1975 - 1976	Thomas R. Godkins, PA-C
1976 - 1977	Roger G. Whittaker, PA-C
1977 - 1978	Dan P. Fox, PA-C
1978 - 1979	James E. Konopa, PA-C
1979 - 1980	Ron Rosenberg, PA-C
1980 - 1981	C. Emil Fasser, PA-C
1981 - 1982	Jarrett M. Wise, PA-C
1982 - 1983	Ron I. Fisher, PA-C
1983 - 1984	Charles G. Huntington, PA-C
1984 - 1985	Judith B. Willis, MA, PA-C
1985 - 1986	Glen E. Combs, PA-C
1986 - 1987	R. Scott Chavez, PA-C
1987 - 1988	Ron L. Nelson, PA-C
1988 - 1989	Marshall R. Sinback, Jr., PA-C
1989 - 1990	Paul Lombardo, PA-C
1990 - 1991	Bruce C. Fichandler, PA-C
1991 - 1992	Sherri L. Stuart, PA-C
1992 - 1993	William H. Marquardt, PA-C
1993 - 1994	Ann L. Elderkin, PA-C
1994 - 1995	Debi A. Gerbert, PA-C
1995 - 1996	Lynn Caton, PA-C
1996 - 1997	Sherrie Borden, PA-C

1997 - 1998	Libby Coyte, PA-C
1998 - 1999	Ron L. Nelson, PA-C
1999 - 2000	William C. Kohlhepp, MHA, PA-C
2000 - 2001	Glen E. Combs, MA, PA-C
2001 - 2002	Edward Friedmann, PA-C
2002 - 2003	Ina S. Cushman, PA-C
2003 - 2004	Pam Moyers Scott, MPA, PA-C
2004 - 2005	Julie Theriault, PA-C
2005 - 2006	Richard C. Rohrs, PA-C
2006 - 2007	Mary P. Ettari, MPH, PA-C
2007 - 2008	Gregor F. Bennett, MA, PA-C
2008 - 2009	Cynthia Lord, PA-C
2009 - 2010	Stephen Hanson, MPA, PA-C
2010 - 2011	Patrick Killeen, MS, PA-C
2011 - 2012	Robert Wooten, PA-C
2012 - 2013	James Delaney, PA-C

PHYSICIAN ASSISTANT EDUCATION ASSOCIATION

Past Presidents

1972 - 1973	Alfred M. Sadler, Jr., MD
1973 - 1974	Thomas E. Piemme, MD
1974 - 1975	Robert Jewett, MD
1975 - 1976	C. Hilmon Castle, MD
1976 - 1977	C. Hilmon Castle, MD
1977 - 1978	Frances L. Horvath, MD
1978 - 1979	Archie S. Golden, MD
1979 - 1980	Thomas R. Godkins, PA-C
1980 - 1981	David E. Lewis, Med
1981 - 1982	Reginald D. Carter, PhD, PA-C
1982 - 1983	Stephen C. Gladhart, EdD
1983 - 1984	Robert H. Curry, MD
1984 - 1985	Denis R. Oliver, PhD
1985 - 1986	C. Emil Fasser, PA-C
1986 - 1987	Jack Liskin, MA, PA-C
1987 - 1988	Jesse C. Edwards, MA
1988 - 1989	Suzanne B. Greenberg, MS
1989 - 1990	Steven R. Shelton, MBA, PA-C
1990 - 1991	Ruth Ballweg, PA-C
1991 - 1992	Albert F. Simon, PA-C
1992 - 1993	Anthony A. Miller, PA-C
1993 - 1994	Richard R. Rahr, EdD, PA-C
1994 - 1995	Ronald D. Garcia, PhD
1995 - 1996	James Hammond, MA, PA-C
1996 - 1997	J. Dennis Blessing, PhD, PA-C
1997 - 1998	Donald L. Pedersen, PhD, PA-C

1998 - 1999	Walter A. Stein, MHCA - PA-C
1999 - 2000	P. Eugene Jones, PhD, PA-C
2000 - 2001	Gloria Stewart, EdD, PA-C
2001 - 2002	David Asprey, PhD, PA-C
2002 - 2003	James F. Cawley, MPH, PA-C
2003 - 2004	Paul L. Lombardo, MPA, PA-C
2004 - 2005	Patrick T. Knott, PhD, PA-C
2005 - 2006	Dawn Morton-Rias, EdD, PA-C
2006 - 2007	Anita D. Glicken, MSW
2007 - 2008	Dana L. Sayre - Stanhope, EdD, PA-C
2008 - 2009	Justine Strand de Oliveira, DrPH, PA-C
2009 - 2010	Ted Ruback, MS, PA-C
2010 - 2011	Kevin Lohenry, PhD, PA-C
2011 - 2012	Anthony Brenneman, MPAS, PA-C
2012 - 2013	Constance Goldgar, MS, PA-C

NATIONAL COMMISSION ON CERTIFICATION OF PHYSICIAN ASSISTANTS

*Past Presidents/Chairmen**

1974 - 1976	Thomas E. Piemme, MD
1977 - 1978	J. Rhodes Haverty, MD
1979 - 1980	Raymond H. Murray, MD
1981 - 1983	Robert B. Bruner
1984	Edmund C. Casey, MD
1985 - 1986	Michael P. Sheldon, PA-C
1987 - 1988	Paul S. Goldstein, MD
1989 - 1990	Stanley R. Shane, MD
1991 - 1992	Hershel L. Douglas, MD
1993 - 1995	Richard Gemming, PA-C
1996	Richard Rohrs, PA-C
1997 - 1998	Marshall F. Sinback, Jr., PA-C
1999	John T. Hayden, MA
2000	Dewayne Andrews, MD
2001	Elaine Grant, MPH, PA-C
2002	Katherine J. Adamson, MMS, PA-C
2003	Gary Winchester, MD
2004	John Ogle, MD
2005	Dorothy Pearson, PA-C
2006	William C. Kohlhepp, DHSc, PA-C
2007	Randy D. Danielson, PhD, PA-C
2008	Lee B. Smith, MD, JD
2009	Edward J. Dunn, MBA
2010	Donald J. Sefcik, DO, MBA
2011	Barbara Barzansky, PhD

2012	Patricia A. Cook, MD
2013	Mark Christiansen, PhD, PA-C

*From 1974 through 1986 the title "President" was used. Changed to "Chairman" 1987-1998; to "President" again from 1999-2002. Became "Chairman" 2003-present.

ACCREDITATION REVIEW COMMISSION ON EDUCATION FOR THE PHYSICIAN ASSISTANT

Past Chairmen

1972 - 1975	Malcolm L. Peterson, MD
1975 - 1978	James A. Collins, Jr., MD
1978 - 1980	Frederic L. Schoen, MD
1980 - 1982	Robert B. Chevalier, MD
1982 - 1984	Frances L Horvath, MD
1985 - 1986	F. Maxton Mauney, Jr., MD
1987	Leland W. Wright, MD
1988 - 1989	Robert N. Curry, MD,MPH
1090 - 1991	David W. Wagner, MS, PA-C
1992 - 1993	Bruce C. Becker, MD
1994 - 1995	Brown R. Manning, MPH, PA-C
1996 - 1997	Laura J, Stuetzer, MS, PA-C
1998 - 1999	Stephanie Bowlin, EdD, PA-C
2000 - 2001	James E. Somers, PhD, PA-C
2002 - 2003	Dana L Sayre Stanhope, MS, PA-C
2004 - 2005	Patricia M. Dieter, MPA, PA-C
2006 - 2007	Gloria M. Stewart, EdD, PA-C
2008 - 2009	Patrick C. Auth, PhD, MS, PA-C
2010 - 2011	James B. Hammond, MA, PA-C
2012 - 2013	James A. Van Rhee, MS, PA-C

PHYSICIAN ASSISTANT HISTORY SOCIETY

Past Presidents

2002 - 2003	J. Jeffrey Heinrich, EdD, PA-C
2003 - 2004	Ron Nelson, PA-C
2004 - 2005	J. Dennis Blessing, PhD, PA-C
2005 - 2006	Ruth Ballweg, MPA, PA-C
2006 - 2007	Pam Moyers Scott, MPAS, PA-C
2007 - 2008	Richard Dehn, MPA, PA-C
2008 - 2009	Ruth Ballweg, MPA, PA-C
2009 - 2010	Carl Toney, PA-C
2010 - 2012	William H. Marquardt, MA, PA-C
2012 - 2013	Thomas E. Piemme, MD

APPENDIX B

APPRECIATIONS TO NATIONAL HEALTHCARE LEADERS

Appreciation is expressed to some of the many leaders from medical specialty societies, academic institutions, government agencies, and foundations, and from within our own ranks, who have championed the physician assistant cause over half a century.

Kathleen Andreoli, DSN, FAAN, a nurse educator, helped Dr. Stead develop the first curriculum used to formally educate PAs at Duke University; served on the first NBME Advisory Board for PA certification and on JRC-PA accreditation site visitor teams. She helped establish a PA Program at the University of Alabama at Birmingham and ended her illustrious career as Dean of the College of Nursing at the Rush University Medical Center, Chicago, IL, in 2005.

Barbara J. Andrew, PhD, was Director of the project to develop the Certifying Examination for the Assistant to the Primary Care Physician at the National Board of Medical Examiners. She developed the template and conducted field trials of testing of physical examination skills of the PA. Later, as Director of Research at the NBME, she led the development of the Computer Based Examination (CBX).

Len Hughes Andruss, MD, after practicing in King City, CA, he was recruited to UC Davis Medical School in 1970 to start a family residency program with emphasis on having physicians work alongside NPs and PAs and to practice in rural areas in collaboration with Mary O'Hara Devereaux, RN, and Virginia Fowkes, RN. He served as a consultant to the Robert Wood Johnson Foundation on primary care training and was a national leader in primary care and rural health.

Martha D. Ballenger, LL.B., coordinated efforts at Duke University to establish model legislation for PAs that made an exception to the Medical Practice Act that allow PAs to work under the supervision of a physician to perform medical tasks without legal reprisal. Legislation was enacted in NC in 1971 and similar legislation soon followed in other states. Currently, she is assistant dean for student affairs at the University of Virginia School of Law.

Timi Agar Barwick joined the staff of APAP (now PAEA) in 1991 and has served as the Association's Executive Director since 2000. Under her direction, the number of PA Member Programs has more than tripled and the organization has developed its own independent management system with major increases in staff and space, a central application process, and a well-attended scientific annual conference.

Jo Ivy Boufford, MD, was active in the 1970's working on the Health Teams Project at Montefiore Medical Center in the Bronx with David A Kindig, MD and Harold Wise, MD. The program was one of the first to demonstrate the importance of health teams in the effective delivery of care. After numerous important leadership positions, she currently is President of the New York Academy of Medicine with a commitment to help New Yorkers lead healthier lives.

Hilmon Castle, MD, was trained as an internist and cardiologist, and also developed a keen interest in Family Medicine and PA Education. He inaugurated both programs at the University of Utah School of Medicine, in the early 1970's and identifies Eugene Stead, Harvey Estes, and Richard Smith as important mentors. He is the only person to serve successive terms as the President of APAP (1974-76).

Jack W. Cole, MD, was Chairman of the Department of Surgery at Yale Medical School in the late 1960's and early 1970's when he obtained a substantial grant from the Commonwealth Fund to improve Emergency Medical Services. He provided invaluable leadership and support to help Alfred and Blair Sadler, Paul Moson and Ann Bliss to develop the PA Program at Yale in 1971. The Yale PA Program Student Society is appropriately named after him.

Mary O'Hara Devereaux, RN, FNP, PhD, while at UC Davis, worked closely with the Stanford PA Program in the 1970's to establish joint training of PAs and NPs under a Robert Wood Johnson Foundation grant. For the past 25 years she has been a leading "futurist," served as a consultant to emerging companies in the U. S. and China and is Founder and CEO of Global Foresight, a San Francisco based strategy consulting firm.

Jesse Edwards, MS, co-founder of the Nebraska University PA Program and former APAP president, 1988-1989, developed the first national computerized test item bank (TIB) used by APAP member PA programs to evaluate their students. He helped establish a joint university/military services PA training program and a distance learning curriculum to award PAs postgraduate master's degrees. Edwards died in 2011.

Joyce Emelio, program specialist for PA Programs, Bureau of Health Professions, Health Resources and Services Administration, Department of Health and Human Services, provided workshops and guidance for Title VII grant applications and oversaw the work of grant reviewers during the 1980s and 1990s. She is a 1994 recipient of the PAEA Outstanding Service Award.

E. Harvey Estes, Jr., MD, former chair of the Duke University's Department of Community and Family Medicine, was influential in the development of model legislation for PAs; the acceptance of PAs by national and local physician and nursing organizations; and the first use of PAs in rural satellite clinics. He brought Stead's vision of PAs to fruition in the 1970s and 1980s. He is the first recipient of AAPA's Eugene Stead Award given in 2009.

Bill Finerfrock served for eight years as the Chief Federal Lobbyist for the American Academy of Physician Assistants from whom he received the President's Award in 2002. An expert on health workforce, rural health, health systems reform and health care financing, he is Vice President for Capital Associates and is the Co-founder and Executive Director of the National Association of Rural Health Clinics.

Virginia Fowkes, RN, FNP, MHS, served as the Stanford PA Founding Program Director and for many years participated in a collaborative effort to train NPs alongside PAs with Mary O'Hara Devereaux, FNP, and Len Hughes Andruss, MD, at UC Davis, initially under a grant from the Robert Wood Johnson Foundation. She has written extensively on decentralized medical learning, primary care and emergency preparedness.

Nicole Gara led the AAPA government affairs department from 1981-2009. Major accomplishments during that time included Medicare coverage, inclusion of PAs in many federal programs, funding for PA education, and commissioned officer status for military PAs. She helped define PA scope of practice by writing model state legislation that emphasized licensure and prescriptive privileges. She forged productive staff relationships with state regulators and organized medicine, and has authored many professional practice and public policy papers.

Anita Duhl Glicken, MSW, is President of the NCCPA Health Foundation. She has 30 years of experience in medical education and is a past president of the PAEA and chair of the PAEA Faculty Development Institute. She is a former director of the Child Health Associate Program, University of Colorado and has been a leader in state, national and international health care initiatives. She is an AAPA honorary lifetime member and recipient of PAEA's Master Teacher Award.

Suzanne Greenberg, MS, the first woman and non-physician to help start and direct a PA Program, served as APAP's first Secretary and Treasurer when it was formed in 1972 and helped guide the organization to prominence. She was president of the organization from 1988 to 1989. She was the profession's longest serving program director when she relinquished her position at Northeastern University in Boston, in 2006. She received APAP's Outstanding Service award in 1992.

Sandy Harding was AAPA's Director of Federal Affairs from 1998 through 2010 and currently serves as AAPA's Senior Director of Federal Advocacy. Through her leadership, AAPA's federal advocacy team has expanded the AAPA Political Action Committee (PA PAC) and AAPA's federal grassroots advocacy capacity. Her advocacy team was successful in passing legislation to create a Director of PA Services in the Department of Veterans Affairs; to increase federal funding for PA educational programs; and to integrate PAs and into the Patient Protection and Affordable Care Act.

J. Rhodes Haverty, MD, Dean of the College of Health Sciences at Georgia State University was the representative of the American Academy of Pediatrics to the National Commission on Certification of Physician Assistants. He served as the Founding Secretary and the second President of the NCCPA. He is one of only three persons to be named an Honorary Commissioner of the NCCPA following his term of office.

Natalie Holt, MD, MPH, wrote an undergraduate thesis "Confusions Masterpiece: The Development of the Physician Assistant Profession" that was published in the *Bulletin of the History of Medicine* in 1998. Based on interviews and primary source material, Holt explored why nursing failed to embrace Eugene Stead's and Thelma

Ingles' 1957 attempt to establish an advanced nurse clinician program at Duke University.

Robert (Bob) Howard, MD, organized three national PA conferences at Duke University; served on study committees to promote the PA concept to medical and nursing leaders; and wrote some of the first articles about PA education and deployment that appeared in leading medical journals and magazines in the 1970s. He cofounded and served as the first president of the American Registry of Physicians' Associates prior to the development of national certification. He died in 2003.

Terrance Keenan was one of the leading philanthropists in health care who helped launch Physician Assistants into American Medicine. At the Commonwealth Fund of New York in the 1960's and at the Robert Wood Johnson Foundation for decades afterwards, he was a strong advocate for the use of PAs and advanced practice nurses working in health teams with doctors to improve primary care. He has been one of the most creative writers about American Philanthropy.

David M, Lawrence, MD, MPH, served as the Director of MEDEX Northwest in the 1970's where he expanded the program and strengthened its curriculum. After serving as Director of Health for Multnomah County, OR, he assumed various leadership roles with Kaiser Permanente and became Chairman of the Board. He now is a health care consultant and is the author of *From Chaos to Cure*.

Margaret E. Mahoney played major roles at several important Private Philanthropies including the Carnegie Corporation, the Robert Wood Johnson Foundation and finally as President of the Commonwealth Fund. She was a strong advocate for innovations in primary care and for the use of PAs and NPs. As a member of the NBME's Goals and Priorities Committee, she advocated for the Board taking on the certification of PAs in the early 1970s.

Denis Oliver, PhD, was director of the PA Program at the University of Iowa for nearly 30 years. While serving as APAP's president from 1984 to 1985, he compiled the *First Annual Report on Physician Assistant Educational Programs* in the United States and continued to do so until 1995. APAP (now PAEA) bestowed upon him their Distinguished Service Award in 1985 for his numerous contributions to the PA Profession. He died in 2010.

Edmund D. Pellegrino, MD, was chosen by Dr. John Hubbard of the NBME to Chair the Advisory Committee on the first national examination for the Assistant to the Primary Care Physician in 1972, which was administered by the National Board the following year. He is Professor Emeritus of Medicine and Medical Ethics at the Kennedy School of Ethics at Georgetown University. Dr. Pellegrino is the recipient of many honorary degrees and awards for his lifetime achievement in medicine and medical ethics.

Henry B. Perry, MD, PhD, MPH, carried out the first extensive survey of the PA profession in 1974 and coauthored *Physician Assistants: Their Contribution to Health Care* published in 1982. The book provided a historical review of the PA profession's development during its first two decades and explored the future use of PAs in the USA. For his significant research of the PA profession, Perry was made an honorary PA by the AAPA in 1985.

Michael L. Powe is vice president of reimbursement and professional advocacy for the American Academy of Physician Assistants. He has a 20-year history of representing the PA profession on issues of health care policy, private third party payment concerns, and Medicare and Medicaid programs. He is the author of the book *Physician Assistant Third Party Coverage.*

Jane Cassels Record, PhD, an economist, conducted studies for over a decade on PAs and NPs working in the Kaiser Permanente Health Plan, Portland, OR. Her studies were the first to describe the use of non-physicians in a health maintenance organization (HMO), the quality of care they provided and the cost-effectiveness of their use. Her book *Staffing Primary Care in 1990: New Health Practitioners, Cost Savings and Policy Issues,* was published by Springer in 1981.

Paul G. Rogers, JD, a Florida Congressman for many terms, was an early champion of the PA profession. He chaired the House Subcommittee on Health and the Environment and served on the board of the Friends of the National Library of Medicine. He was very active in development of the Title VII legislation that helped fund early PA programs, working closely with the founders of the Utah University PA Program, Bill Wilson and Hilmon Castle. He died in 2008.

Richard G. Rosen, MD, employed PAs at Montefiore Hospital to determine their substitutability as surgical house staff to reduce the number of surgeons being educated in the USA. Subsequently, he helped launch the country's first postgraduate surgical residency program for PAs at Montefiore Hospital in 1973. He served as an AAPA advisor and wrote articles and delivered papers at surgical conferences promoting the use of PAs in surgery. He became an AAPA honorary member in 1976.

C.H. William Ruhe, MD, PhD, held a long tenure as Director of the Department of Medical Education of the AMA. He oversaw the development of *Essentials for Educational Programs for the Assistant to the Primary Care Physician*, and provided leadership for the formation of the Joint Review Committee on Accreditation. He was an acknowledged national leader in Continuing Medical Education.

Blair L. Sadler, JD, in collaboration with his twin brother Alfred, was instrumental in recommending amendments to State Medical Practice Acts to allow PAs to practice in the late 1960's while working as a health policy analyst at the NIH. He helped found the Yale PA Program in 1971 and with Alfred Sadler and Ann Bliss is the coauthor of *The Physician's Assistant: Today and Tomorrow*, published by Yale Press in 1972, and underwritten by five Foundations.

Richard Scheffler, PhD, one of the first economists and health care policy fellows to study the potential impact of PAs on US health care, conducted his first national study in 1972. The study described the role and practice characteristics of 150 PAs. Since then, he has researched, written articles, testified and served on national workforce panels advocating for policy changes necessary to fully realize the benefits of health care team practices.

Eugene S. Schneller, PhD, author of *Physician's Assistants: Innovation in the Medical Division of Labor* published in 1978, was the first sociologist to analyze the newly emerging PA profession, which he felt, at the time, was a significant innovation in the medical division of labor. Schneller coined a new term, "performance autonomy," to describe how PAs advance their careers, unlike that of any other health professional, through negotiation, knowledge and skill development.

David Sundwall, MD, trained as a primary care physician, served as director of the health staff of the U.S. Senate Labor and Human Resources Committee and supported Title VII funding for PA educational programs during the 1980s. After 24 years in various government and private sector health positions in Washington, D.C., he returned home to direct the Utah Department of Health (2005-2010). He received the PAEA Outstanding Service Award in 1993.

Malcolm C. Todd, MD, was Chair of the AMA's Council on Health Manpower during the formative period of the PA profession. He convened the 14 organizations that formed the National Commission on Certification of Physician Assistants. He was President of the AMA during the implementation of Medicare and Medicaid.

William (Bill) Wilson, PhD, a co-founder and first director of the Utah University MEDEX (PA) Program, coordinated efforts to establish federal funding for emerging PA programs from the Bureau of Health Manpower, DHEW. He worked closely with Paul G. Rogers, US Congressman from FL, and with Dr. David Sundwall, staff director of the US Senate Labor and Human Resources Committee, to assure continued funding during the 1970s. He died in 2010.

SELECTIVE BIBLIOGRAPHY

JOURNAL REFERENCES:

Carter, RD., Thompson, A. People v Whittaker: The Trial and Its Aftermath in California. *The Journal of Physician Assistant Education*. 2008;19(2):44-51.

Estes, EH and Carter, RD. Accommodating a New Medical Profession: The History of Physician Assistant Regulatory Legislation in North Carolina. *NC Med J.* 2005;66(2):103-107.

Fine, L.L.; Silver, H.K. Comparative Diagnostic Abilities of Child Health Associate Interns and Practicing Pediatricians. *The Journal of Pediatrics* 83, no.2:332-335. August 1973.

Gifford, JF, Jr. Prototype PA. *NCMJ*. 1987;48(11):601-603.

Holt, N., Confusion's Masterpiece: The Development of the Physician Assistant Profession. *Bull.Hist.Med.* 1998;72:246-278.

Hooker, R., Carter, R., and Cawley, J. The History and Role of the National Commission on Certification of Physician Assistants. *Perspective on Physician Assistant Education*. 2004;15(1):8-15.

Hudson, CL. Expansion of medical professional services with nonprofessional personnel. JAMA. 1961;176:839-841.

Komaroff, AL., W.L. Black, WL, et. al., Protocols for Physician Assistants: Management of Diabetes and Hypertension, *New England Journal of Medicine.* 1974;290:307-312.

Sadler, A.M. Jr.; Sadler, B.L. Recent Developments in the Law Relating to the Physician's Assistant. *Vanderbilt Law Review*; 24, no. 6:1193-1212. November 1971.

Silver, HK, Ford, LC, Stearly, SG. Program to Increase Health Care for Children: The Pediatric Nurse Practitioner Program. *Pediatrics*, 1967;39:756-760.

Silver HK, Ott JE The child health associate: a new health professional to provide comprehensive health care to children. *Pediatrics.* 1973; 51:1-7.

Smith, RA., Bassett G, Markarian C, et.al. A strategy for health manpower: reflections on an experience called Medex. JAMA. 1971;217(1):1362-1367.

Sox, H., Tompkins, R. The Training of Physician's Assistants: The Use of the Clinical Algorithm System for Patient Care, Audit of Performance and Education. *New England Journal of Medicine*, 1973;288:818-824.

Stead, EA, Jr. Conserving costly talents - providing physician's new assistants. JAMA. 1966;198(10):182-

BOOK REFERENCES:

Ballweg R, Sullivan EM, Brown, D, Vetrovsky D, eds. *Physician Assistant: A Guide to Clinical Practice.* 5th ed., Philadelphia, PA: Elsevier Saunders, 2013.

Carter, RD, Perry, HB, eds. *Alternatives in Health Care Delivery: Emerging Roles for Physician Assistants.* St. Louis, MO: Warren H. Green, 1984.

Hooker RS, Cawley JF, Asprey DP. *Physician Assistants: Policy and Practice,* 3rd ed., Philadelphia, PA: FA Davis, 2010.

Ingles, Thelma M. *Care from the Heart.* Edited by Susan Haradon. La Mesa, CA: BTW Publishing, 2012.

Lippard, V., Purcell, E. eds. *Intermediate-Level Health Practitioners.* New York, NY: Josiah Macy, Jr. Foundation, 1973.

Myers, HC. *The Physician's Assistant: A Baccalaureate Curriculum.* Parsons, WV: McClain Printing Company, 1978.

Perry, HB, Breitner, B. *Physician Assistants: Their Contribution to Health Care.* New York, NY: Human Services Press, 1981.

Record, JC. *Staffing primary care in 1990: physician replacement and cost savings.* New York, NY: Springer Pub. Co., 1981.

Sadler, AM, Jr., Sadler, BL, Bliss, AA. *The Physician's Assistant Today and Tomorrow: Issues Confronting New Health Practitioners.* (2nd Ed.) Cambridge, MA: Ballinger Publishing Company, 1975. (Available as free download on PA History Society Website at http://pahx.org/pdf/SadlerSadlerBliss2ndEd.pdf)

Schneller, E. *The Physician's Assistant: Innovation in the Medical Division of Labor.* Lexington, MA: Lexington Books, 1978.

Zarbock, SF., Harbert, KR. eds. *Physician Assistants: Present and Future Models of Utilization.* New York, NY: Praeger Publishers, 1986.

Index of Names

About the Authors

Thomas E. Piemme, MD, is Emeritus Professor of Health Care Sciences and Medicine at The George Washington University. He is the former Chair of the Department of Health Care Sciences, and Associate Dean for CME. He is a Past President of PAEA, and of NCCPA. He is currently President of the Physician Assistant History Society. He is retired and lives in Phoenix, AZ.

Alfred M. Sadler, Jr., MD, was Founding Director of the Yale PA Progam, Founding President of PAEA, coauthor of the first policy book about PAs and served as a Senior Officer of the Robert Wood Johnson Foundation, all in the 1970's. For the past 32 years has practiced primary care medicine in Monterey County, CA, where he has worked with and precepted PAs and NPs. He is President Elect of the PA History Society and lives in Carmel, CA.

Reginald D. Carter, PhD, PA, is the former Chief of the Division of Physician Assistant Education in the Department of Family and Community Medicine at Duke University. He is a Past President of PAEA. He was the founding Executive Director, and is currently the Historian Emeritus of the Physician Assistant History Society. He is retired and lives in Mebane, NC.

Ruth Ballweg, MPA, PA-C, is Professor and Director of the MEDEX Northwest Physician Assistant Program in the Department of Family and Community Medicine at the University of Washington. She is a Past President of PAEA and of the Physician Assistant History Society, which she currently serves as Historian. She is a recipient of the Eugene A. Stead Award from the AAPA. She lives in Seattle, WA.